JAW-10-69

# Exercises in Linguistics

## by A. E. Darbyshire

EDWARD ARNOLD (PUBLISHERS) LTD.
LONDON

© A. E. Darbyshire, 1968

*First published 1968*

SBN: 7131 1124 0

PRINTED IN GREAT BRITAIN BY
WESTERN PRINTING SERVICES LTD., BRISTOL

# Preface

The aim of this book is to supply a series of exercises which may be
helpful for those who want to understand something of the methods
of linguistics and would like to do so by using English as the language
of exemplification. Each set of exercises is introduced by a short description
of the kind of topic dealt with in it, and thus the book is, in some
sort of way, self-contained. But a fuller account of the main principles
and ideas should, ideally, be found in other sources. For this reason
references are given, on page vi, to the author's *A Description of
English*. More advanced students might also like to consult Professor
Barbara M. H. Strang's *Modern English Structure*.

At all times the method is synchronic, and no considerations of the
diachronic study of language are included. Almost all the material in
the exercises has been taken from contemporaneous sources—newspapers,
periodicals and books published in Britain since 1960. These
exercises are not intended to be exhaustive, and they can be supplemented
by recourse to similar kinds of material; the comparative
analysis of such material is, by the way, a very useful critical exercise.

In a book such as this there are bound to be technical terms, and some
of them may be new to some readers. However, no new technical
term is introduced without immediate definition, either here or in *A
Description of English*, and where a new meaning is given to an old term
it is explained. It has been thought best to sketch only lightly the
phonetic and phonological aspects of linguistics of English in this
book—not because they are not important, but because information
on these topics is easily available in Britain, and British scholars have
done excellent work in developing such studies among us. It is thought
rather that the more neglected aspects of linguistic theory in popular
exposition in this country should be given more emphasis.

A. E. D.

iii

# Contents

|  |  | page |
|---|---|---|
| | Preface | iii |
| 1 | Communication | 1 |
| 2 | Language | 4 |
| 3 | Linguistics | 7 |
| 4 | Speech Mechanism | 10 |
| 5 | English Phonemes | 14 |
| 6 | Structure | 18 |
| 7 | Types of Structure (I) | 22 |
| 8 | Types of Structure (II) | 26 |
| 9 | Transforms | 30 |
| 10 | Linguistic Analysis | 34 |
| 11 | Functional Contrasts | 37 |
| 12 | Functors and Lexemes | 40 |
| 13 | Immediate Constituents | 43 |
| 14 | Grammaticality | 47 |
| 15 | Segmentation | 51 |
| 16 | Nominal Segments (I): Position | 55 |
| 17 | Nominal Segments (II): Structure | 59 |
| 18 | Form-classes (I) | 63 |
| 19 | Verbal Segments | 67 |
| 20 | Form-classes (II) | 70 |
| 21 | Morphology (I) | 73 |
| 22 | Morphology (II) | 76 |
| 23 | Lexis | 80 |
| 24 | Idiolect, Dialect, Register | 84 |
| 25 | Stylistics | 87 |
| | Some Applications | 91 |
| | Index | 121 |

The following tabulates the interrelation between the chapters in this book and the sections within chapters of *A Description of English* for those using the latter as their basic text:

1  I: 2, 6, 7, 8, 10, 11
2  I: 13, 14, 15, 16, 17
3  I: 3, 4, 5;  II: 18, 19, 20
4  III: 35, 36, 37, 38
5  III: 37, 39, 40, 41, 42, 43
6  II: 24, 25;  III: 51, 52
7  II: 26, 28;  III: 51, 52, 53
8  II: 24, 26, 27, 28;  III: 51, 52, 53, 55, 56  *paradigmatic*
9  III: 56, 57, 58                                *syntagmatic*.
10  II: 27, 28, 29, 30, 31;  V: 77
11  II: 27, 28, 29, 30, 34
12  II: 30, 31, 32;  IV: 54, 55, 64, 65
13  II: 26, 27, 28, 29, 30
14  II: 19, 20, 21; IV: 47
15  II: 24, 25, 31, 32;  IV: 49, 51, 54, 55
16  IV: 54, 55, 59, 60, 61, 62, 66, 67
17  IV: 54, 55, 59, 60, 61, 62, 65, 68
18  II: 24, 26;  VI: 54, 64, 65, 68
19  IV: 53, 54, 56, 57, 58, 61, 62, 65, 72, 73
20  IV: 61, 63, 65, 66, 74
21  IV: 69, 70, 71, 73, 74
22  IV: 57, 58, 72
23  V: 75, 77, 78
24  I: 6, 7, 8, 9, 13, 14, 15, 16
25  V: 76, 77, 79, 80, 81

# Chapter 1

# Communication

**Communication** can be defined as the transference of information from one system to another. The act of communication implies that there must be at least two systems, and that they must be in a stimulus-response relationship. (The word *system* is used here to make the definition perfectly general. In communication by means of language, of course, there is chiefly the transference of information between human beings, and sometimes between human beings and animals trained by them. But there are other communication methods than language.)

Communication can take place only by means of a code. A **code** is a pre-arranged set of signs. A **sign** is a physical mark or event that conveys information; and **information** is an instruction to make a choice from the signs of a code. For example, the letters of the alphabet that you see on this page are signs, and as you can see by looking at them, they have different shapes. These different shapes tell you how to distinguish one from another, that is, each different shape carries different information enabling you to choose what that shape means and to reject what the other shapes might mean. When letters are assembled to form words, the same sort of thing happens, so that words are signs too. And so, for that matter, are words assembled into sentences.

When communication takes place, an **encoder**, or the system originating a message, chooses a number of signs from a code, assembles them in some kind of order, and thus makes a **signal** or the physical embodiment of the message. This signal acts as a stimulus to cause a **decoder**, or the system to which the message is sent, to respond in some way. If the decoder understands the **message**, or the meaning of the signal, the response is the making of a selection from the items of the same code in accordance with the instructions carried by the information in the signs which make up the signal.

Usually the systems concerned in sending and receiving messages are living things or parts of living things, for communication can exist at a variety of levels, as when cells (or parts of them) convey genetical information from parent to offspring, or as when one part of a nervous system sends information to another, or as when animals communicate with one another by means of sounds, smells, colours, movements of the body, etc., or as when human beings communicate and share experience with one another by means of the spoken and written word, or pictures, sculpture, maps, diagrams, bells, flashing lights, dancing, music, drama, and so on.

Sometimes machines have built-in communication devices put there by human beings, as in computers in which parts can 'give instructions' to other parts, or as in servo-mechanisms by means of which designed responses of certain parts of the machinery can be controlled.

Language is the chief means of making signals used by human beings. A language is a code with a very large number of signs which are capable of making an infinite number of signals in the physical form of speech (**phonic substance**) and, very often, writing (**graphic substance**).

## Exercises 1

1 'A sign is a physical mark or event that conveys information directly. Thus, if I see a black cloud on the horizon, I say that it is a physical event which is a sign of rain; or if, driving my car, I hear an unusual noise coming from the engine, I say that the noise is a physical event which is a sign that something is wrong. A symbol, on the other hand, is a physical mark or event which conveys information indirectly. A symbol represents or stands for something other than itself. Thus a fish was a symbol to the early Christians, or a hammer and a sickle make a symbol for communists.'

Discuss these definitions and find other examples.

Refer to examples of the following and decide in what ways they can be said to be signs or symbols or combinations of signs which make symbols or combinations of symbols:

the vocal sounds of speech; the letters of alphabets; the figures and marks used in mathematics; chemical formulae; gestures; the ringing of bells; graphs; tables of statistics; still and moving photographs; smoke signals in the Arizona desert; numbers on or near the front doors of houses; drumbeats in the Congo jungle; traffic lights; dress; flags; dancing; scenery or the sets and lighting during the performance of a play; the movements of pointers over dials as with clocks or speedometers.

2 'Thoughts, beliefs, opinions, emotions, and all that goes on in the brains and nervous systems of individuals, are private and cannot be examined directly. Therefore, if we want to study the communications made by people, the only way available to us is the examination of the physical embodiments made by the communication channels that people use. We can only know what is going on inside a person, so to speak, by looking at what is happening outside. If a person laughs, we conclude he is happy; if a person weeps, we decide that he is sad.'

Discuss this notion. Provide examples of the physical embodiments of various communication channels that you can think of. What scientific instruments are available or imaginable for measuring and comparing them? Is the quotation above true of all communication channels you can think of, or is it only true of those used by human beings?

Look up the word *person* in a good dictionary. Examine its history. Why, do you think, does the author of the quotation say 'so to speak' after the expression 'inside a person'?

3 'The symbols H and C on the taps in a bathroom are a simple code.'

Explain this statement, and refer to the stimulus-response situations likely to be encountered in relation to those symbols.

Assemble details of various codes, e.g., a library classification scheme, the method of numbering rooms in a large building, a telephone dialling system. Discuss the ways in which they work.

4 Consider such simple devices as an electric front door bell, the ball-and-cock tap in a domestic hot water supply, or a thermostat. Describe how they work, and discuss whether such devices can be said to provide communication channels.

# Chapter 2

# Language

The word *language* could be defined as follows: **Language** is a complete articulatory system of arbitrarily symbolic vocal sounds used by human beings for communication and sharing experience. This definition may not appeal to all linguists, but it does at least provide a starting point. The best way to understand it is to take it bit by bit, starting at the end and working backwards.

The expression *for communication and sharing experience* shows that language is social. It exists among groups of people, called **speech-communities.** A means of communication invented by one person for communicating with himself would not be a language as linguists understand the word.

The words *used by human beings* show the limits of what linguists are interested in in their professional moments. Language is only one kind of communication method among many others.

The words *vocal sounds* show the kind of means of communication linguists study. The sounds produced by the human vocal organs are the basis of language as the linguist understands it. Writing, although of course very important, is largely an attempt to record speech, and even writing as communication in its own right, as in, for example, newspapers, periodicals or textbooks, is based upon the spoken word and symbolizes what could be, or has been, spoken.

The words *arbitrarily symbolic* describe the nature of the vocal sounds that are the basis of language. Groups of the sounds of a language symbolize or stand for men's ideas of things in the actual world of things and in men's imaginations. The word *arbitrarily* shows the way in which vocal sounds are symbolic. There is no special connexion or necessity between what words stand for and the words themselves. Different languages—and also the same languages—use different words or signs to symbolize the same things.

The words *articulatory system* show the kind of thing that a language

4

is—a whole made up of a complexity of parts. And the word *articulatory* shows that these parts are not separate, but that they work together. One of the most important properties of a language is its power to build up larger units out of smaller ones, so that the larger units function in an entirely different way from the smaller.

The word *complete* shows that at any given time the number of parts that make up the language system is sufficient for the speech-community that uses it. For example, the word *radar* is part of English, yet before radar was invented English-speaking people had no need to use the word *radar*, which became part of English only when the necessity for it arose. This does not mean to say that every language has a word (or some other means of symbolizing) everything, but merely that members of speech-communities can symbolize by means of their language as much as they want to.

# Exercises 2

**1** Given the words *eat, Japanese, fish, melts, of, ice, sun, the, plenty*, it is possible in English to construct such utterances as 'The sun melts the ice' or 'The Japanese eat plenty of fish'.

Why are such constructed orders of words as those intelligible to speakers of English, while such constructed orders as '*plenty the the fish ice' or '*Japanese the of' or '*of eat of' are not intelligible? (The symbolic asterisk * occurring before a constructed set of words or a linguistic form is used to show that it is a made up one and not found in actual usage.)

**2** Human beings can construct out of the elements of language utterances that have never existed before but which can be immediately understood by other human beings who know the language. Why cannot the word *language* be applied with scientific accuracy to the utterances of such birds as parrots or budgerigars which can imitate human speech?

**3** Consider, after adequate preparation by means of reference to books on animal behaviour, the relationship of human speech to such forms of animal behaviour as the dancing of bees, birds' songs, the movements of wolves, gibbon calls, and so on.

**4** It is well known that what in British English are called *tap*, *pavement*, *biscuit* and *lift* are in American English called *faucet*, *sidewalk*, *cookie* and *elevator*, or that German bells go *bim-bam* while English bells go *ding-dong*.

Make lists of other examples, either known to you or discoverable, of the arbitrary symbolism of language.

**5** A man whose name is William Smith may be called William, Will, Bill, Billy, Mr Smith, Smith, sir, daddy, darling, or 'that man over there' or 'the man in the grey overcoat', and so on, each different word or expression referring to the same man.

Consider and report on, after adequate preparation and the collection of sufficient examples, the ways in which the names given to people might vary with relationships of kinship and social standing and the circumstances of the speaker or writer of the name.

Can you find examples of a similar sort of indication of relationship or attitude of mind in the names given to animals, plants, places or things?

**6** Compare and contrast the following definitions of the word *language* with that given on page 4:

'Language is nothing but a set of human habits, the purpose of which is to give expression to thoughts and feelings, and especially to impart them to others.' (*Otto Jespersen*)
'A language is a form of speech of which any workable description can be made.'
'A language is a system of conventional signals used for communication by a whole community.'
'Language is a purely human and non-instinctive method of communicating ideas, emotions and desires by means of a system of voluntarily produced symbols.' (*Edward Sapir*)
'Language is the expression of ideas by means of speech-sounds combined into words.' (*Henry Sweet*)

# Chapter 3

# Linguistics

Linguistics can be thought of as the scientific study of language in all its aspects. In such an expression as *the scientific study of language* the word *language* is used as a name for a class of things and not for any one thing in particular. Except as a concept, or tool of analysis, there is no such thing as language. In the non-analysed reality of the world there are only languages—English, French, Russian, Japanese, Fijian, Eskimo, Hittite, and so on.

The study of language can be either **diachronic** or **synchronic**. The first is historic, tracing the development of a language through a period or periods of its growth. The second is descriptive of a language at a particular period of time. The course of study attempted here is a synchronic description of British English in the second half of the twentieth century.

Whichever method is undertaken, the student will have to examine something of the following seven branches of linguistics:

1) **Phonetics:** This is the study of the vocal sounds used by speakers of languages.

2) **Phonology:** This is the study of the sounds used by speakers of a particular language, and the ways in which they function as contrastive elements in making combinations of them meaningful. Generalized conceptions of the sounds of a particular language are called **phonemes,** and these can be regarded, for most purposes, as the smallest elements of the language system.

3) **Morphology:** This is the study of the behaviour and meaning of linguistic units called morphemes. The word *morpheme* may be defined as the minimal grammatical unit.

4) **Syntax:** This is a study of the ways in which morphemes pattern into structures in the use of a language. *Structures* are groups or arrangements of morphemes ordered in special ways according to the conventions of the language in which they occur.

7

5) **Lexicography:** This is the study of the *lexis*, or the total stock of the morphemes of a language, with descriptions of the ways they are used, or their *function*, their meanings, and sometimes their histories.

6) **Semantics:** This is the study of the concept of meaning, and of the ways in which the morphemes of a language become meaningful in their use or function. Strictly speaking, semantics belongs to a wider range of disciplines than linguistics, since the concept of meaning must also occur in other means of communication than language; but, clearly, the linguist must take into account the idea of meaning.

7) **Stylistics:** This is the study of the ways in which individual speakers and writers of the language use it, taking into account such ideas as those of *register*, or language considered in relation to its use.

# Exercises 3

**1** 'Explain why there is no such thing as a mammal.'

Has this instruction any meaning? Is there any sense in which it can be said that, although the idea represented by the word *mammal* is very useful in science, there are actually no mammals in the world but only animals with mammalian characteristics?

List and explain the usefulness of any similar kinds of words you know —*metal* and *acid*, for instance. Do such words as *pressure*, *temperature*, *valency*, *ratio*, *velocity*, etc., behave in the same kind of way?

**2** Why is it necessary for scientists to insist on exact definitions?

The principle of definition used in this book is as follows: the predicate (in the sense of the word as used in formal logic) of the definition gives, first, the class of things to which the thing whose name is being defined belongs, and second, its differentia or the way in which it differs from other things of the same kind or class.

'The **referent** of a word or expression is the thing or idea symbolized by that word or expression.'

Does this definition of the word *referent* meet the requirements of a good definition? Examine other definitions so far given in this book and criticize them (that is, assess their value) with the same criteria in mind.

**3** Suppose that the definitions, (1) 'A pig is a farmyard animal reared for the production of pork, ham, bacon, lard, chitterlings, bristles, pig-skin, etc.', (2) 'A pig is an ungulate bristle-bearing non-ruminant omnivorous mammal', and (3) 'A pig is a thing like that filthy thing over there', are all true, how do you reconcile their differences to their truth? If, in another book on linguistics, you came across a different definition of the word *morpheme* from the one given in this book, how would you decide which was right or if both were wrong, or would you allow the possibility that both could be right?

'You can only give a definition of a word, never of a thing that a word may stand for.'

What is your opinion of the truth or otherwise of this statement?

**4** 'In the scientific study of language it is clearly necessary to have a metalanguage. A **metalanguage** is a group of words, all strictly defined, used by an impartial observer for describing a natural object-language, that is, any ordinary language or dialect in which the observer is interested.'

The words given on pages 7 and 8 above are some of the words that could constitute a metalanguage for the description of a natural language like English. But if English is a natural language, in what ways can the vocabulary of a metalanguage be said to be non-natural or artificial? How can such a metalanguage be operated inside English?

'The sounds represented by the symbols *p*, *b*, *k*, *g* are phonemes of English.'
'The sounds represented by the symbols -*s* and -*es* at the ends of some words in English and denoting plural forms are English morphemes.'

What words in those two sentences can be said to be part of a meta-language of linguistics? What words are not part of the metalanguage? Are there any words in the two sentences which might be described as borderline cases?

Is a metalanguage necessarily composed entirely of technical terms? What about such words as *the*, *a*, *an*, *of*, *is*, *are*, etc.?

# Chapter 4

# Speech Mechanism

As we have said, the sounds produced in the human respiratory tract are the basis of language as the linguist understands it. Normally, most people learn to speak before they learn to write, and the vast majority of human beings who have lived on the Earth have never learnt to write and read at all. Writing is a secondary linguistic activity which attempts to record—sometimes very inefficiently—the sounds of speech, and writing becomes a means of communication in its own right only among highly civilized peoples.

**Speech-sounds** are vibrations in the atmosphere produced by the respiratory tract of the human body. The source of energy needed to make these sounds is provided by the lungs and some of the muscles of the upper part of the body. The lungs expel air through the larynx, the pharynx, the mouth and the nose. (See diagram on page 11.) In these four places the air-stream expelled from the lungs is modified in various ways, and these modifications cause the realization of phonic substance and the qualities of the different speech-sounds.

The sounds so produced can be described according to the ways in which the air-stream is modified. There are two great classes of speech-sounds, vocoids and contoids. The **vocoids** are those speech-sounds which are produced when the air-stream is allowed free passage, without audible friction, and when the organs of speech create resonance—in English this is brought about by various positions of the tongue and lips making changes in the inside shape of the mouth. The **contoids** are those speech-sounds produced when two or more of the movable parts of the vocal organs obstruct the passage of the air-stream, completely or partially, so as to produce audible friction. In **phonetics**, which is the science which studies the speech-sounds produced in all the languages of the world, the vocoids are usually described in terms of the positions of the tongue and lips, and the contoids in terms of their place of articulation, or parts of the vocal organs that make them,

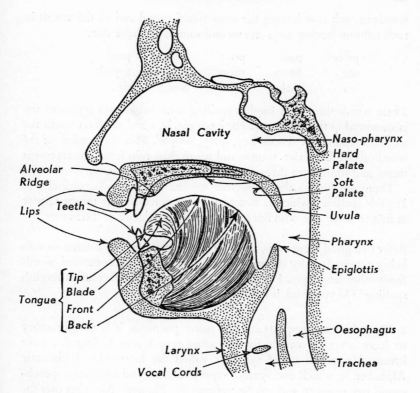

Nasal Cavity

Naso-pharynx

Hard
Palate

Alveolar
Ridge

Soft
Palate

Lips     Teeth

Uvula

Pharynx

Epiglottis

Tip
Blade

Tongue

Front
Back

Oesophagus

Larynx

Vocal Cords

Trachea

and the kind of stricture, or kind of partial or complete closing of the
air passage.

# Exercises 4

**1** Cats purr. The 23rd psalm. That's what I saw. The frigate put out to
sea. Please pass. My sister Sue. The captain stood on the poop. Gold,
frankincense and myrrh. Chocolate mousse. Please may I have some
more? He wants that piece. Show it to me. The planet Mars. The rich
and the poor. No, sir.

If we list the last words of these fifteen expressions so that we have
three rows of five words and five columns of three words, with all the

words in each row having the same initial sound and all the words in each column having the same second sound, we have this:

| piece | pass  | poor | poop   | purr  |
|-------|-------|------|--------|-------|
| me    | Mars  | more | mousse | myrrh |
| sea   | psalm | saw  | Sue    | sir   |

These words show that English spelling does not always represent the same sound in the same way. For example, *ie, e* and *ea* all represent the second sound of the words 'key, quay, people'. Moreover, some of the words above have two sounds and more than two letters to represent them, and some have three sounds and four or five letters.

There are historically explicable reasons for these discrepancies in English spelling, which is not really so inconsistent as might appear at first to some one who has no historical knowledge of the matter.

Refer to a good dictionary, and find more examples of the same sound's being represented by different symbols. English has borrowed words from other languages. How, do you think, does this fact affect English spelling? Do you think it should?

**2** Since, in some respects and for many purposes, it is unsatisfactory to have several symbols for the same speech-sound, linguists have invented a special set of symbols, called the International Phonetic Alphabet, in which one symbol represents one, and only one, speech-sound (see pages 16 and 17). Sometimes this Phonetic Alphabet uses the same letters as the Roman alphabet, and sometimes different ones. For instance, the initial sounds of the fifteen words listed in **1** in phonetic notation are /p,m,s/.

In phonetic symbols the words *heap, heart, hoard, who, heard* are /hiːp, haːt, hɔːd, huː, hɜːd/. As you can hear when you say aloud these words to yourself, there is only one symbol for each sound: /ː/ is to be counted as one symbol for /ː/ indicates that the sound represented by the symbol preceding it is long.

Given this information you can now transcribe all except one of the speech-sounds of the fifteen words given in **1**. Do so.

The sound you cannot transcribe so far is the last sound of *Mars* which is not the same as the last sound of *pass* or *piece*. The phonetic symbol for the last sound of *Mars* is /z/. This sound appears in such words as *haze, maize, zoo, zebra* /heɪz, meɪz, zuː, zebr *or* ziːbr/.

How many English words can you now express in phonetic notation? Write them as you say them, not as you think they ought to be said.

**3** Perhaps you do not pronounce *pass* with the second sound the same as in *Mars* or *psalm*. Perhaps you pronounce it with the second sound the same as in *cat* or *fat*. That does not matter. The pronunciation given here is what is called **Received Pronunciation (RP)**, which is generally taken to be the pronunciation of educated speakers of South-Eastern British English. It is a dialect of English generally given in books on English phonology (see page 7), arbitrarily chosen as 'standard' by those who teach English to foreigners, and by those who think that they know what is 'correct' pronunciation. A variant of it, 'BBC English', is understood over the whole of Britain.

Discuss the idea of correctness in pronunciation, and the view that no kind of pronunciation is *linguistically better or worse* (though socially it may be) than any other.

Chapter 5

# English Phonemes

Not all the very vast number of sounds that the human vocal organs are able to make are heard in all languages. English-speaking people, for instance, find it hard to utter the last sound of the French words *la rue*, because that sound does not appear in English, and English-speaking people do not use it naturally. Frenchmen, on the other hand, find it hard to pronounce the initial sound of the English word *thick* /θik/, because that sound is never heard in French.

It is obvious that a speech-sound, when uttered in ordinary, everyday speech, exists only for a very short time, a fraction of a second, and that no two repetitions of what we think of as the same sound will, as a matter of fact, be precisely alike when considered from the acoustical point of view. Certainly no two speakers are likely to produce the same sound in all circumstances. Yet when we hear people speak and repeat words they have already used, we imagine we are hearing the same sounds. The differences are so small we discount them.

Generalized conceptions of the sounds of a language are called its **phonemes**. Phonemes can be thought of as families of sounds, each of the members of which are so nearly alike that they seem to be alike and are thought of as being alike. Individual sounds which are members of a phoneme are called its **allophones**. For instance, the English phoneme / r /, as in *run, Mary* or *mirror*, is heard as a roll in some Scottish dialects and as a flap in some southern English pronunciations.

The function of phonemes is to be **contrastive**. In such a series as *pan, pen, pin, pun* there are six phonemes of English represented by the letters *a, e, i, u, p, n*. In each of the words two phonemes, represented by *p* and *n*, are the same. Therefore the only way we have of knowing that *pan*, say, is different from any other word in the series is by the fact that the phoneme represented by *a* contrasts with that represented by *e* or *i* or *u*.

When we speak of the phonemes of a particular language, we do not,

14

as a rule, use the words 'vocoid' and 'contoid', but **vowel** and **consonant**.

The vowels and consonants of English occur mingled together in examples of connected speech, but they do not occur anyhow or in random combinations. They occur together in units called **syllables**, which show, to a certain extent, what is called **stability**, that is, they appear again and again made up of the same parts. If V symbolizes 'vowel', C symbolizes 'consonant,' and C$^c$ 'consonant cluster', then we find in English such recurring forms as V, CV, C$^c$V, VC, VC$^c$, CVC, C$^c$VC, CVC$^c$, C$^c$VC$^c$ and C, as exemplified by the words *a*, *my*, *sky*, *am*, *ask*, *hat*, *stop*, *post*, *strength*, and (*cott*)*on*. But we are not likely to find such syllable patterns as CC or VV.

# Exercises 5

**1** The phonemes of a language can be discovered by means of what is known as **commutation** or the discovery of **minimal pairs**, that is, pairs of syllables in which one is contrasted with the other by only one sound. Arrays of syllables in which one sound is successively changed horizontally and vertically can be productive of phonemes in this way:

| Pete | pit | pat | pert | pet | pan | pain | pine | pawn | pin |
|------|-----|-----|------|-----|-----|------|------|------|-----|
| beat | bit | bat | Bert | bet | can | cane | kine | corn | kin |
| bean | bin | ban | burn | Ben | cat | Kate | kite | caught | kit |

It must be remembered that any syllable introduced into any list or array must be reliably authenticated by being heard in actual speech.

Starting with the list *pin*, *bin*, *kin*, *tin*, *din*, *chin*, *gin*, *fin*, *thin*, *sin*, *shin*, *win* as the left-hand column of an array, see how many English phonemes you can produce.

**2** Experiment with various combinations of English syllables, and then answer these questions, using your own pronunciation:

Is the sound heard in the first syllable of *about* the same as that in the last syllable of *better*? Does this sound also appear in words like *opposite*, *doctor*, *pleasure*, *immediately*? What minimal pair establishes this sound?

What consonants never appear at the beginnings of syllables?

What consonants never appear at the ends of syllables?

Are there any words in English in which the medial consonants of words like *measure, leisure* occurs at the end?

What is a diphthong?

**3** The following list contains fifty words. There are 44 different English phonemes. Choose from the list the minimum number of words which will give examples of (a) 12 vowels, (b) 8 diphthongs, (c) 2 semi-vowels, and (d) 22 consonants:

ring, judge, show, calm, meat, witch, go, kill, thinking, pleasure, full,

## THE INTERNATION
(Re

|  |  | Bi-labial | Labio-dental | Dental and Alveolar | Retroflex | Pa alv |
|---|---|---|---|---|---|---|
| **CONSONANTS** | Plosive . . . | p b |  | t d | ʈ ɖ |  |
|  | Nasal . . . | m | ɱ | n | ɳ |  |
|  | Lateral Fricative . . | | | ɬ ɮ | | |
|  | Lateral Non-fricative . | | | l | ɭ | |
|  | Rolled . . . | | | r | | |
|  | Flapped . . . | | | ɾ | ɽ | |
|  | Fricative . . . | ɸ β | f v | θ ð \| s z ɹ | ʂ ʐ | ʃ |
|  | Frictionless Continuants and Semi-vowels | w ɥ | ʋ | ɹ | | |
| **VOWELS** | Close . . . . | (y ʉ u) | | | | |
|  | Half-close . . . | (ø o) | | | | |
|  | Half-open . . . | (œ ɔ) | | | | |
|  | Open . . . . | (ɒ) | | | | |

(Secondary articulati

like, see, mill, moon, pit, butter, earth, thought, here, put, church, zoo, toy, no, poor, day, buy, vase, men, yellow, Tom, cow, like, then, church, boy, caught, pot, nice, sat, there, poor, kind, bit, say, knot, wet, tap, bought

**4** Experiment with various consonant clusters, as in such words as *plague, blame, scratch, twelfth, whisker, whelks.* Which clusters can appear at the beginnings of syllables and which only at the ends of syllables. Classify according to the number of consonants in the kinds of clusters.

**5** Can you transcribe the following words in phonetic notation?

stethoscope, diocesan, trachometer, psittacine, pteridology, pseudonymous, sthenic, prosopopoeia.

# IONETIC ALPHABET.
1951.)

| lveolo-<br>palatal | Palatal | Velar | Uvular | Pharyngal | Glottal |
|---|---|---|---|---|---|
| | c ɟ | k g | q ɢ | | ʔ |
| | ɲ | ŋ | ɴ | | |
| | ʎ | | | | |
| | | | ʀ | | |
| | | | ʀ | | |
| ɕ ʑ | ç j | x ɣ | χ ʁ | ħ ʕ | h ɦ |
| | j (ɥ) | (w) | ʁ | | |

| Front | Central | Back | | |
|---|---|---|---|---|
| i y | ɨ u | ɯ u | | |
| e ø | | ɤ o | | |
| | ə | | | |
| ɛ œ | | ʌ ɔ | | |
| æ | ɐ | | | |
| a | ɑ ɒ | | | |

n by symbols in brackets.)

# Chapter 6

# Structure

If we examine the following utterance, taken from a magazine article on archeology,

'The floors were found covered with kitchen refuse, and burnt patches where braziers had stood could still be clearly seen',

we can see that it contains two parts, that each part represents a different idea that the author wanted to express, and that the two parts are separated by the word *and*. We can think of each of these two parts as an example of the class of things called **sentences**, even though it may be difficult, at the moment, to define the word *sentence*. However, most people whose native language is English would be able to recognize that such forms of words as 'The floors were found covered with kitchen refuse' and 'Burnt patches where braziers had stood could still be clearly seen' are examples of the kind of things they would call sentences. We can also see that these two utterances are of the same form, or structural pattern, and it is because of this that they are examples of the kind of things called sentences. We can test for ourselves that they are of the same form or structural pattern by taking parts out of one sentence and substituting them for parts of the other, e.g.:

'The floors could still be clearly seen'
'Burnt patches where braziers had stood were found covered with kitchen refuse',

and in both cases we can recognize in the form or the pattern the kind of thing we call a sentence.

How far can we go with this technique of substitution? Clearly if we go too far there will be some combinations of parts which we shall be able to recognize only as nonsense: e.g., '*still could with burnt the' or '*had with seen stood braziers floors'.

It is obvious that we cannot be indiscriminate in our choice of those parts we take for substitution, and that we must have some kind of control over what we are doing. This control can be at first a **semantic** one, that is, one concerned with meaning. A native speaker, or **informant**, if we refer to one, could tell us that some forms of words are meaningful and others are meaningless. But the linguist must himself check this kind of meaningfulness. We must be clear about the sense in which these words, *meaning*, *meaningful* and *meaningless*, are used. It has nothing to do with belief or truth. For instance, a man might not believe in fairies and he might say that to him such an utterance as 'There are fairies in the wood' is meaningless. That is not the sense in which *meaning* is used here. Although we may not believe that the utterance 'There are fairies in the wood' is true, we can nevertheless understand the structure of it, because we can compare it with other utterances of a similar form or pattern which we know to be true and believable, such utterances, for instance, as 'There are books in the library', 'There are houses in the village', 'There are people in the street'.

In this way we can distinguish between **referential meaning**, or the ordinary everyday sense of the word meaning, and **formal meaning**, which is intelligibility of structure without, necessarily, intelligibility of reference. With formal meaning we can understand that the words of a particular form make sense, although we may not understand what they refer to.

# Exercises 6

**1** Given the following parts of the two sentences in the utterance on page 18, construct out of them as many intelligible sentences as you can:

the floors                burnt patches
were found                where braziers had stood
covered                   could still be clearly seen
with kitchen refuse

Can any words be taken out of any of these parts and other words from other parts substituted for them? For instance, *kitchen* could be taken out of *with kitchen refuse* and *burnt* put in its place. Why, do you think, will some words but not others go in some places to produce structures that would satisfy an informant?

**2** The following fifteen sentences are taken from newspapers and periodicals printed in Britain since 1960. Parts are marked off with solidi. Construct at least forty other sentences by means of substitution of parts. In each case verify the structure you have made by reference to an informant.

(a) The bowlers of Sussex / had / their moments.
(b) A model without electronic phasing / is / also available.
(c) Some stockbrokers / send / circulars to their clients.
(d) While they were waiting, / Margot / told / the inspector / what she had done.
(e) Such holiday resorts / have / everything you want.
(f) Overnight / she / became / famous.
(g) Yesterday / he / drove to the farm entrance.
(h) The police / are seeking / information about the yacht.
(i) The couple / have / a fortnight's holiday.
(j) Understandably, / the unions / have refused / to go to arbitration.
(k) Many farmers / condemned / the offer.
(l) The boys / elected / him / the captain of their team.
(m) Black paint / is / cheap.
(n) Every Sunday / they / came to the park.
(o) The young newly-weds / arrived in their new car.

**3** It is clear that some of the parts or segments of the sentences in **2**, have the same form or structural shape or pattern as others, and that some are of different patterns. For instance, some segments consist of one word and some of more than one, and segments like *the police* or *the couple* or *the boys* have a common pattern.

a) Classify as far as you can all those segments which have a common structure in the fifteen sentences above.

b) Is it possible to take out of the larger word-group segments smaller segments which have a common pattern? If so, do so.

c) The following are some of the segments divided into two classes: Class I—*is, are, became, came, arrived*; Class II—*had, send, have, condemned, are seeking*. Can you explain, without taking into account any grammatical knowledge you may have acquired before reading this book, the difference between the kind of items found in Class I and those found in Class II?

d) Using all or some of the items in the two classes in c) above, construct sentences of three parts or segments on the models of (a) and (m) in **2**. Which sorts of segments cannot follow Class I items and which sort cannot follow Class II items and satisfy an informant?

e) Is there any difference that you can explain between the first three items in Class I in c) and the last two items in Class I?

f) Construct, first, sentences of two segments, second, sentences of three segments containing as a second segment one of the first three items of Class I of c), third, sentences of three segments containing as a second segment one or two of the items of Class II of c), fourth, sentences of four segments on the model of (d) without the first segment *While . . . waiting*, and, fifth, sentences of four segments on the model of (1).

Can you explain the differences among the five types of sentences thus produced?

g) What do you notice about the following segments? *While they were waiting*; *Overnight*; *Yesterday*; *Understandably*; *Every Sunday*.

Put these segments in different positions in the sentences in which they occur and notice the differences that result.

# Chapter 7

# Types of Structure (I)

The following five sentences can be constructed from some of the parts
of sentences given in 6:2 1) He / arrived; 2) They / are / the police; 3)
They / condemned / the offer; 4) She / told / him / what she had done;
5) They / elected / him / captain. There are two criteria by which we
can establish a method of describing and classifying such parts of sentences as these, and therefore sentences themselves. The first criterion
depends on meaning. The kinds of things or ideas that become the
referents of some words or word-clusters are different from the kinds of
things or ideas that become the referents of others. Thus, we know
because we understand the meanings of English words, that words like
*arrived*, *are*, *condemned* and *told* have referents of a different kind from
words or word-clusters like *he*, *the police* or *what she had done*. But this
criterion is not always satisfactory or reliable, because it does not
always take into account the formal meaning of sentences or their
segments. Two sentences such as 'They are the police' and 'They are
famous' have the same form because *famous* and *the police* are interchangeable segments, but from the point of view of ordinary everyday
meaning *famous* and *the police* do not have the same sorts of referents.
The second criterion, linguistically more reliable, depends on what are
called **formal characteristics**. We can have such a sentence as 'They
told the police' or 'They are famous', but not such a sentence as '*They
told famous'. Thus we can see that 'They told the police' is a different
sort of sentence from 'They are famous', and that *the police* is a different
sort of segment from *famous*.

One of the formal characteristics of English sentences is the position
of segments. Such segments as *he*, *she*, *they* are likely to occur before
such segments as *condemned*, *arrived*, *told*. Some segments can come after
*is*, *are* but not after *condemned*, *told*, *elected*, while after such a segment as
*arrived* no segment of the five sentences above that can come after
these others fits at all.

We can give the name **groups** to those segments into which the sentences above are divided, and define a **group** as one or another of six constituent parts of possible English sentences without at least one of which no English sentence can be constructed.

Although the criteria for the formal establishment of groups will have to come later, we can set out the names of the groups and the positions which they normally occupy in the five basic English sentence types as follows:

1) subject / intransitive verb
2) subject / intransitive verb / complement
3) subject / transitive verb / object
4) subject / transitive verb / indirect object / object
5) subject / transitive verb / object / complement.

The six kinds of groups indicated above could be symbolized as follows: S, I, C, T, O, $O_2$ (indirect object). Upper-case letters are used because we may want lower-case letters to symbolize smaller units. The five sentence types are, symbolically, SI, SIC, STO, $STO_2O$, and STOC.

# Exercises 7

1 One of the formal characteristics of English sentence structure is that groups usually (though not always, of course) occur in a definite order. Most languages have what is called a 'favourite sentence type', and in English it is that of *actor-action*. That is, the subject (S) usually comes first, and then the verb (I or T) comes next, and then the complement (C), if there is one, or the object (O), if there is one, comes after that. This is a general statement of what happens most often; there are of course occasional exceptions. Our knowledge about this favourite sentence type or pattern comes from our informant, because we can go to him with a large number of sentences whose groups have been jumbled up, and we can go on 'unjumbling' them, gradually getting nearer and nearer to an acceptable order of groups until the right one appears. It is, of course, a long and tedious process, but it can be done, and so far as this book is concerned we shall assume that it has already been done.

Consider the following sentences. Identify the groups, which are separated by solidi. Classify the sentences according to type, and express symbolically. (All the sentences are taken from newspapers and periodicals printed in Britain since 1960.)

a) They / say / their own business is being damaged. (b) I / met / such a man. (c) This / is / Bach at his warmest and most appealing. (d) Heavy rains at the end of last month / will increase / supplies of autumn and winter vegetables. (e) She / considered / him / an amiable fool. (f) Those / could be / famous last words. (g) Cleopatra / was / the Queen of Egypt. (h) This article / will show / you / how to make your talents pay. (i) Thousands / flocked to the market place. (j) Helen, who had momentarily looked up from her sewing, / quietly shook / her head. (k) The Committee / starts from the basis that there already exist two separate methods of securing consumer protection, one statutory and the other voluntary. (l) The duration of the convention / is / fifty years. (m) Farm workers / have / good reason to worry about their future. (n) A photo-electric cell connected to a galvanometer / provided / a means of measuring the density of each section of the iris. (o) The fact that there is already in summer time substantial congestion on the approach roads / is / evidence not of a need to retain the railways but of the rate of transference of traffic to the roads.

It will be noted that the number of groups in the sentences of each type is always the same, no matter how many words any particular sentence might contain.

**2** From a study of sentences of SIC and STO types can you deduce what the difference is between a complement and an object? Is it merely that an object follows a transitive verb and a complement doesn't? And can we say that a transitive verb is by definition one that is followed by an object, and that an intransitive verb is by definition one that is not followed by an object, but which is either not followed by another group or by a complement? Is to argue thus to argue in a circle?

With SIC sentences it is sometimes possible to transpose the subject and the complement. Thus, both the sentences 'Henry VIII was the king' and 'The king was Henry VIII' would satisfy an informant. But is this kind of transposition always possible with STO sentences to an informant's proper satisfaction? What about the two sentences 'The sun melts the ice' and 'The ice melts the sun' or 'John plays golf' and 'Golf plays John'? Can the second of either of these pairs of sentences satisfy an informant in the same way as the first can? The second has formal meaning in each case, but could it have referential meaning? Is it possible to have a sentence which is formally meaningful and referentially meaningless?

**3** Such questions as those given above are not so silly or unimportant as they may appear at first sight. For one could argue that if linguistics is to be of any value in the society in which it is studied, then it must not only provide a static description of the language and leave matters at that, but it must also be of some dynamic use in telling people what are acceptable sentences in that language and what are not, so that it could be applied, say, in the education of the young who need to know how to express themselves, or in the teaching of the language to foreigners. Discuss these ideas.

# Chapter 8

# Types of Structure (II)

We have now to see what justification there is for the assertions made in Chapter 7. If examples of the sentence types set out in the last paragraph are examined, it can be seen there are sixteen group positions distributed among five sentences. Let us symbolize these positions by numbers:

1. 1 / 2
2. 3 / 4 / 5
3. 6 / 7 / 8
4. 9 / 10 / 11 / 12
5. 13 / 14 / 15 / 16.

We have now to look at the words or word-clusters from an actual sample of sentences, say those of **6/2**, see how they fit into the numbered places, and find out what kinds will fit and what kinds will not. However, we need not take a very large number of words or word-clusters, because we can see that such words as *he / she / they / him* will correlate with a large number of groups. For example, *they* will correlate with *The bowlers of Sussex* or *Many farmers*; *she* with *Margot*; *him* with *the inspector*. Operating, therefore, only with these four words will make things simpler.

In this manner, we can see that *he / she / they* can always stand in subject positions (1, 3, 6, 9, 13), but never in transitive or intransitive verb positions (2, 4, 7, 10, 14), or in object positions (8, 11, 12, 15). However, they can occur in complement position (5), as in such SIC sentences as 'These are they' or 'It was he / she who told me'. In some such way as this, after we had assembled and experimented with groups from a very large number of groups from a large sample of sentences, we could determine that subjects are different from verb and object groups but not always different from complement groups.

There is also a formal characteristic of verb groups that sets them apart. A very large sample of verb groups would show that their heads (see page 28) would provide variant forms. In such a series, or **paradigm**, as *arrive | arrives | arrived | arriving*, we find that the endings can be repeated in another series such as *condemn | condemns | condemned | condemning*. If we took a very large sample of verbs we should find that all of them could have the ending *-s* or *-ing*, and many of them could have *-ed* as well, and *-s* always appeared on verb-forms that came after *he | she | it* as subjects, or groups for which *he | she | it* could be substituted. This formal characteristic is only found among verbs and is enough to set them in a class by themselves.

We can define a **subject** as a group which typically precedes a verbal group and which can be replaced by one of the forms *I | he | she | it | we | you | they*. We can define a **verbal group** as one which typically follows a subject, and which can be replaced by the form *am | is | are+ base + ing*. We can define a **transitive verb group** as one which is typically followed by an object. We can define an **object** as a group which typically follows a transitive verb and which can be replaced by one of the forms *me | him | her | it | us | you | them*. We can define an **intransitive verb group** as one which can either stand by itself after a verb or be followed by a complement. We can define a **complement** as a group which typically follows an intransitive verb or an object in STOC sentences.

# Exercises 8

**1** We are now in a position to give a provisional definition of the word *sentence*. We could say that a **sentence** is a linguistic form containing one or another of a certain arrangement of groups.

We could further qualify 'certain arrangement' by saying that it is syntagmatic. By **syntagmatic** we mean occurring in a definite order, which we can describe as being of a sequence in time or space. When sentences are spoken they occur in time, and have definite beginnings and ends at definite moments of time. When they are written down they occur in space, and English sentences are normally written down in linear order from left to right, with the parts in the same order in space as they would be in time if spoken. This order is important in English since it can become contrastive. We know, or an informant can tell us, that the sentence 'George hit Harry' is a different one from

'Harry hit George' only because of the order in which the parts occur. This order is the contrastive element that signals the difference. In some languages, Latin for instance, this is not so; in Latin *Puer amat puellam* is exactly the same sentence as *Puellam amat puer* or as *Puer puellam amat*.

If the definition above is worth anything, it follows that, no matter how many words a sentence may contain, it will have only a known number of groups, either two, three or four. It is possible, for instance, for an SI sentence to have only two words, 'Swallows migrate', but it is also possible to expand this sentence by putting more words in it without increasing the number of groups, e.g., 'The swallows that come to Europe in the spring migrate annually to Africa at the end of the European summer.' Here *The swallows that come to Europe in the spring* is the subject group (S), and *migrate annually to Africa at the end of the European summer* is the intransitive verb group (I).

In most cases, groups which contain more than one word can be made up of what are called **heads** and **adjuncts**. In the SI expanded sentence given above, the word *swallows* is the head of the subject and *migrate* is the head of the intransitive verb. All the other words make adjuncts of one kind or another.

Classify the following sentences according to type. Express symbolically. Discover and identify heads by substitution in subjects, objects or complements of *I | he | she | it | we | you | they* or *me | him | her | it | us | you | them*, and apply the extra check of position in doubtful cases where *you* or *it* might occur. Notice formal characteristics of heads of verbal groups.

(a) The new ship will have a hydraulically-operated bow door which will lead to a much faster turn-round in port. (b) The rules of the I.M.F. actually include machinery for altering the international value of gold by uniform adjustments in exchange parities. (c) The tungsten carbide business has had a difficult year by reason of the widespread reduction in activity in the engineering industry. (d) A more basic question to which the Seven could start giving serious attention is their own relationship with the rest of Europe. (e) These encouraging signs, which the Chancellor noted last month, have occurred before the Government's intervention could be felt. (f) The hotels which accommodate this, and sooner or later, almost every other conference, take a cautiously impartial view of political affiliation. (g) The opposition of United States industrialists could be dangerous to the success of any agreement reached when it comes to the stage of Congressional ratification. (h) A vicar hit back yesterday at parishioners who complained because his pretty blonde wife wore slacks at a church bazaar. (i) Such visco-moters are useful for determining the viscosity of molten metals, of liquid hydrogen, of liquid helium, and for investigating the dynamic rheological properties of materials, especially those which are unable to support their own weight. (j) The use of nitrocellulose lacquer allows colours of exceeding brilliance to be produced.

**2** Consider sentences (d), (f), (g), (j) of exercise 6/2. If the segments *While they were waiting, Overnight, Yesterday* and *Understandably* are left out, the remaining groups are enough to make intelligible sentences and to determine sentence type. These segments can be called **sentence-adverbs,** and they obviously have an influence on the whole of the sentence in which they occur. Find and discuss other examples, change their positions in their sentences and note differences.

# Chapter 9

# Transforms

Many sentences of type STO, STO$_2$O and STOC, which contain transitive verbs and therefore objects, have the property of being capable of being expressed in different form. Examples in the column on the left are in one form and those in the column on the right are in another:

Swallows eat insects.              Insects are eaten by swallows.

Mother gave me sixpence.  { I was given sixpence by mother.
                          { Sixpence was given me by mother.

They made him manager.             He was made manager by them.

The three sentences on the left are said to have their verbs in the active voice, and the four on the right are said to have their verbs in the passive voice. The linguistic concept of **voice** may be defined as a form of a verb which indicates the relationship of the referent of the subject to the referent, or 'action' of the verb. We can say that the **passive voice** is a form of the verb in which any exponent of that form is a past participle preceded by a finite form of the verb *to be*.

(It must be remembered that the word *action*, as used above, is used in its technical sense here to mean simply 'the referent of the verb', although what the referent is need not be specified, and indeed linguistically is not always important. In such an utterance as 'Queen Anne is dead', no action at all, in the non-linguistic sense of the word, is referred to; but in the same non-linguistic sense, very violent action is referred to in such an utterance as 'Brutus stabbed Caesar'; yet from the linguistic point of view both *is* and *stabbed* are verbs, and linguistically both refer to action.)

We can now add to our list of sentence types four more, of which examples are given in the right-hand column of the first paragraph of this Chapter. These four sentence types can be symbolically represented as SPA, SPO$_2$A, SPOA and SPCA, where P stands for 'passive verb group' and A for 'sentence adverb'. Very often in the use of the language it will be found that the use of A, which is of course an adverbial phrase, is omitted in passive sentences.

It should be noted that not all transitive and active sentences can be made passive. Such a sentence as 'He resembles his father', for instance, is hardly likely to have a passive transform.

The passive form of sentences can be generated from the active, or the active from the passive, if we know either. All we need to do is apply certain rules and we can make either into the other. This idea leads to the conception of what is sometimes known as **transformational grammar**, which is a method of describing language by transforming some sentences into others. There is no need merely to transform active into passive or vice versa. We could apply the technique to sentences of the same form. If we have a set of sentences which we have decided are 'grammatical', that is, conforming in some way to some agreed principles of sentence construction in some language or dialect, then we can generate other grammatical sentences from these by obeying certain rules. If we could work out some kind of symbolism, as in algebra, we could generalize these ideas and thus account for every possible grammatical sentence capable of being uttered in the language.

# Exercises 9

**1** Devise a set of rules for transforming active sentences into passive and passive ones into active.

**2** Classify the following sentences according to type, express symbolically, and identify heads and adjuncts of groups.

(a) The costing of BEA fares works on the zone system (like taxi fares in Washington, DC). (b) The fears expressed by the Labour Party about re-investment in electricity undertakings are not justified by the figures recently published. (c) In most tropical countries the ratio of doctors to the population is only one-fifth to one-hundredth that of Britain. (d) In the comfortable bars, the lounges, the cinemas—everywhere, people are loving this luxury voyage to New York. (e) The problem of machine design is further complicated by the shapes of the glass containers chosen for their sales value. (f) Standards are prepared by the use of sodium silicate solutions of known silica content. (g) Valuable lessons in hospital function and design were learnt by the team which studied the numerous experiments already carried out in the United States and Canada. (h) The present chairman of the company was elected to the Board as long ago as 1939. (i) The effects of other phosphates were studied only briefly as these were felt to be of only minor importance. (j) At the same time, while wage-rates are being increased, a corresponding increase in profits is not being maintained.

3 Consider carefully each of the following utterances, classify them into classes on some principle you are able to explain, and then write an account of the ways in which they differ from any of the sentences already dealt with.

(a) Is it true that the West is morally bankrupt? (b) When will these politicians come to their senses? (c) Halt major road ahead. (d) Do these people imagine that they will succeed? (e) Compare these new policies with those put forward last year. (f) How can people really like to have plaster gnomes in their front gardens? (g) Gone are the days of crude, amateurish treatments. (h) There are three main reasons for this state of affairs. (i) It is noticeable that the Gaelic of the Outer Hebrides is crisper and sharper than that of the Inner Isles. (j) A more sympathetic audience no one could wish for. (k) There are many aspects of this complicated affair still to be accounted for. (l) Why have they failed to agree? (m) Has modern science pushed too far ahead of the man in the street? (n) It is not often realized how few physical properties of a material are relevant to a particular industrial application. (o) Where do we go from here?

4 In what ways are questions and commands (imperatives) different from statements? Can you explain why there are no subject groups in commands (imperatives)?

5 Collect examples of sentences with the words *there* and *it* in subject positions. What, if anything, is the 'real' subject, as distinct from the linguistic subject, of such sentences? For instance, in such a sentence as 'It is well known that people tell lies' what is the status of *that most people tell lies*? Does the transform of that sentence, 'That most people tell lies is well known' express the same idea as well, better, or not as well?

**6** Can you find examples of sentences in which the normal order of groups is inverted or changed, as (g) in 9/3? What is the value of such an inversion from the point of view of the author of the sentence and from the point of view of the hearer or reader of it?

# Chapter 10

# Linguistic Analysis

In Chapters 6, 7, 8, and 9 we have been dealing with linguistic structures which we have called sentences. All the examples of sentences given in the exercises are real specimens taken from periodicals and newspapers printed in Britain since 1960. But none of them is complete. Each is part of a larger structure—a paragraph, and that paragraph is part of a still larger structure, an article, a report, a short story.

The normal method of linguistic analysis is to take a large linguistic structure—usually called a **chain of discourse** or **discourse**—and gradually break it down into smaller and smaller components, until one comes down to the smallest linguistic unit of all, the phoneme. Such a method is long and laborious, and is only really necessary when it is desired to make a record of some unfamiliar or unwritten language. With a language such as British English, of which there is an abundance of written samples of hundreds of different kinds—from traffic signs in the street to whole libraries of a variety of fact and fiction—a great deal of the breaking down into components has already been done by the writers themselves, or at least, by the printers who have set standards of punctuation and presentation, so that we can easily go to some printed document to pick out a sample of some kind of English usage and say, 'That is the sort of thing I mean by a chapter, a paragraph, a sentence, a word, or whatever'.

We have already seen that sentences are structures of groups, and that groups are made up of words. A group may consist of a single word or a number of words. From this one might conclude that sentences could be analysed into groups, and the groups then analysed into words, and that would be the end of the matter. Unfortunately things are not quite so simple as that. What, for instance, is a word? Because we are familiar with the printed word—a group of letters of the alphabet with a space before and after—we think we know what a word is. In one sense, of course, we do, because most of us have no difficulty in deciding where to put the spaces when we write words. But the division of stretches of language into the kinds of things we are able to recognize in a conventional way as words is quite arbitrary and artificial, and does not necessarily correspond to other facts that can be discovered by means of linguistic analysis.

As we have already said, language is fundamentally a series of vocal sounds, and the method we have of recording these sounds in writing or graphic substance has developed over the centuries into a means of communication in its own right, with its own techniques and conventions. Because in this country most of us are familiar with writing, our knowledge of the written word has influenced our thinking about the spoken word, so that our ideas of what—to borrow a phrase from physics—we might call the fundamental particles of language is not always very clear.

It is the purpose of linguistic analysis to elucidate the facts of language from a study of the actual uses of language and to make clear how a language is constructed.

## Exercises 10

1 The following is a transcript of part of a tape-recorded conversation by some young people on the topic of the use of leisure. In the course of the conversation some one suggested that we ought to be paid for what we do in our leisure time and give up some of our time to work unpaid for the community as a whole. The transcript takes up part of the discussion from there. Christine and Malcolm were two participants.

The transcript is presented in normal English spelling, but as a continuous flow, with pauses marked by solidi. One solidus means a short pause, two solidi mean a longer pause, three solidi mean a longer pause still. The paragraphing denotes different speakers.

'wellIthink / mostpeople / intheirleisuretimedon'tdoanything / whichgives / givesanythingtosocietyasawhole // thereforethey / shouldn'tbepaid // youmightaswell / youcan'tgetpaidforreadingabook-forinstance / becauseitdoesn'tdoanythingforanyonegenerally // unless-you / youwriteanotherbookabout / howyou'vereadthisbook // Ishouldsay / Malcolmshouldgetpaid // quiteabitforhisrecitalsattheArt-GalleryorChristineforputting / Christineforputtingonlipstickand-brushingherhair / butthatdoesn'tdoanythingforsociety / verymuch

'butChristinedoesn'tmakeherselfbeautiful / forthestateasawholedoes-she // Imeanshe'snota / atouristattractionoranythinglikethat

'evenwhenIdogo / andplayattheArtGalleryforinstance / er // Idon't /
Idon'tthinktheycouldgivemethemoneyIreallydeserver /// considering-
alltheyears / andpracticeI'veputin // sometimes / overthreeorfour-
hoursadayfortenyears / Idon'tthinktheycould / er / possiblygivemethe-
sameamountofmoneyasIactuallydeserve // inaccordancewiththe / the-
hardlabourthat's / goneintothe / thefinishedproduct
  'yesbut / theycouldgiveyoumoremoneyif / otherpeople / were-
workingfornothing
  'Idon'tfollow
  'nothepointisthat / everybody'sworking / infactoriesfornothing //
presumablythere'snocapitalism / sowhere'sthestategoingtogetallthe-
revenuefromthepeoplethat / are / thepeoplethatareworking / sothey've-
gotmillionstogiveyou
  'yesbut / thereis / therearepeoplelikeYehudiMenuhinwhoare / who-
aremuchmuchbetterthanIamhowmuch / howmuchareyougoingto-
paythem
  'moremillions'

1) Can you suggest any reason why the following should not be
regarded as single words in English?
'Ithink, mostpeople, forinstance,Idon't, yesbut, thereis, thereare'
2) Bernard Shaw spelt words like *don't, can't, isn't* without an apos-
trophe. Can you justify his practice? Or do you think it is a bad
practice and ought not to be justified?
3) The suffixes *-er, -est* as in *simple, simpler, simplest* are not considered
as separate adverbs in the same way as *more* and *most* as in *beautiful,
more beautiful, most beautiful.* Can you suggest any reasons why they
should not be?
4) In English words like *the, a, an, his, her, its, their* are almost always
followed by a noun or an adjective + a noun. Why should they not be
considered as prefixes like *dis-* or *un-*?


2 Suppose that English were a foreign language to you and that you
were in the process of learning it, and that the transcript above was
written in a phonetic notation you had invented for the purpose of
recording English speech-sounds. How would you decide from a study
of it which segments were English words?


3 What does the transcript tell you about the differences between
written and spoken English?

# Chapter 11

# Functional Contrasts

We have already said that phonemes are contrastive, that, for instance, in such a series as *pan / pen / pin / pain / pine / pun*, we know that any word is different from any other only because of the second phoneme. This principle of contrast is found almost anywhere we care to look in language. For example, consider the two sentences 'George hit Harry' and 'Harry hits George'. First, there is in each sentence the contrast of position of the words *George* and *Harry*. In the first sentence we know *George* is the subject because it comes before the verb, and that *Harry* is the object because it comes after. In fact, it is only because of the contrasted positions of *George* and *Harry* in each case that we know which is subject and which is object—only position, in these cases, can give us that information, and unless we unconsciously had the knowledge that in English sentences position can do this neither of the sentences would be intelligible. Secondly, the absence of a final *-s* after *hit* in the first sentence can contrast with its presence in the second. This is a contrast in the form of the word *hit*. The contrast *hit/hits* in combination with—and this is important—either *George* or *Harry* as subject indicates the time of the event or 'action' relative to the time of its being reported.

It is obvious that groups are contrastive. Not only are they normally contrastive because of their meaning, but they are functionally contrastive because of their position. This idea of function is the link between the semantic aspect, or that of referential meaning, and the form or formal meaning of structures. If different groups are contrastive, it follows that sentences of different types, which are made of different groups, are also contrastive.

Taken together, the ideas of functional contrast and of substitution can lead us to a technique of linguistic analysis which has proved to be very useful in increasing our understanding of language and how it works. If any linguistic structures are examined, and parts taken out to leave places for other parts to be put in, with successively smaller and

37

smaller units, only certain kinds of parts will be found to go in certain places so as to produce intelligible results. If we can ask, and having asked answer some such question as 'Why those certain kinds of parts and not others?' then we have discovered something about the language we are dealing with and can advance towards a description of it. Moreover, this description, if we have applied the technique correctly, can be scientifically accurate, because the technique is objective. It can give us a means of analysis which as far as is humanly possible cuts out the whims and fancies of individual analysts.

## Exercises 11

1 Consider the following extract from a book on language which has after it another, not necessarily better, way of expressing the same ideas:

'Our ignorance about the fundamentals of language is not solely derived from wilful prejudice, natural inertia, or national apathy. Most of our school teaching of language is amateurish and incompetent; many a sixth-form boy can read Racine with ease but have difficulty in asking a gendarme the way to the Metro.' (Anthony Burgess, *Language Made Plain*, London, 1964)

'We are ignorant about what is fundamental in language not because our sole derivation of linguistic knowledge is wilful prejudice, the inertia of nature, or because we are an apathetic nation. Most of what is taught us about language in school is the work of incompetent amateurs; many a sixth-form boy who can read Racine easily may find it difficult to ask a gendarme the way to the Metro.'

Using only the information given in this book, and ignoring any grammatical knowledge you may previously have acquired, explain the contrasts in the following word-pairs:
ignorance, ignorant; fundamentals, fundamental; solely, sole; derived, derivation; natural, nature; apathy, apathetic; amateurish, amateurs; asking, to ask; difficulty, difficult; with ease, easily.

2 Without referring to, or bothering with, or using the technical terms of, any grammar or grammatical knowledge you may have

acquired before reading this book, explain the contrasts in the following pairs:

1) They are here.
   They were here.
2) The men arrived.
   The man arrived.
3) We were considering.
   We were considered.
4) We did that.
   I did that.
5) All those books.
   All these books.
6) I told him.
   I told them.
7) The fish is fresh.
   The fish are fresh.
8) The cats eat fish.
   The cat eats fish.
9) These tall trees.
   That tall tree.
10) We decided.
    I decide.

**3** The contrasts that have been dealt with above can be described as morphemic. A **morpheme** is the smallest meaningful grammatical unit of a language. It may be a word or a part of a word, and it is always contrastive in some way or another. It is clear from this that groups, and therefore sentences, are structures of morphemes.

In the following sentences, unless they coincide with the normal boundaries of the English printed word the morphemes are separated from their neighbour morphemes by hyphens. Examine these sentences and explain in what ways the morphemes are contrastive.

(a) The bowler-s of Sussex had their moment-s. A bowler of Surrey had his moment. (b) Two native-s of Manchester became novelist-s. A native of Liverpool became a pop-singer. (c) It display-s all the characteristic-s of an artefact of Stone Age culture. They display all the characteristic-s of be-ing manufacture-d in Italy. (d) The delegate-s could not take their wive-s with them. The candidate has tak-en his wife with him. (e) Many manufacturer-s are seek-ing new market-s for these kind-s of goods. This manufacturer has sought a new market for this kind of goods.

# Chapter 12

# Functors and Lexemes

If we examine such a sentence as 'The bowlers of Sussex had their moments' we can see that it is a sentence of type STO, and that *The bowlers of Sussex* is the subject group, *had* is the transitive verb group, amd *their moments* the object group. The morphemes in these groups are contrastive at two levels, which we might call the **lexical** and the **formal** or **grammatical**. The lexical meaning of a word or morpheme is that meaning which is shown by a possible referent such as we should find in a dictionary or work of reference. The formal meaning of a word or morpheme is the structural significance it has in a sentence or other linguistic structure in which it occurs. Thus for the words *bowlers* and *Sussex* we can find quite definite referents, but words like *the* and *of* are devoid of meaning in this sense; they are words used in sentences to deal with other words.

Thus, on the lexical level, groups considered as structures of words or morphemes, contrast with other groups with other referents. The group *The bowlers of Sussex* is a collection of words which indicates what the writer of the sentence in which it occurs wants to talk about, and it could contrast lexically with other groups, such as, say, *the fielders of Essex*, or *the forwards of Chelsea*. But these semantic contrasts are only shown by the words *bowlers, fielders, forwards, Sussex, Essex, Chelsea*. The words *the* and *of* and the final *-s* indicating the plural are unchanged.

Just as our symbolic notation of SI, SIC, STO, etc. symbolizes in a general way certain sentence-frames into which all kinds of words can be put according to what people want to say, so some such arrangement as *the . . .-s of . . .* can become a kind of sub-structure frame that could occur in a large number of sentences; in fact it could very easily be the basis for a very large number of subjects, complements or objects. Thus the morphemes *the, of* and *-s*, along with many others, can be said to serve as structural signals to indicate the form of the utterance in which they occur and to define more closely the mere generality of the meanings of other words.

In such an expression as *the bowlers of Sussex*, the words *bowlers* is the **head**, and *the* and *of Sussex* are **adjuncts**. One of the functions of the formal morphemes is to provide the frames of structures in which the relationships of **modification** among heads and adjuncts can be displayed, as in this case the morpheme *of* displays the relationship between the referent of the word *bowlers* and that of the word *Sussex*, so that in the referential meaning of the whole sentence the decoder or reader will know which bowlers are being talked about.

Such considerations as these can lead us to the notion that in English there are two kinds of morphemes. The first kind, which we can call **functors**, consists of those morphemes like *the*, *of* and *-s*, which have no referential meaning in themselves (though they can acquire it when used in utterances) but which function in sentences as structural signals to form the meaning of the structure as a whole. The second kind, which we can call **lexemes**, consists of all those morphemes or words which do have referential meaning, which are arranged in structures by functors, and whose relationships can be displayed by functors.

# Exercises 12

1 Distinguish between the lexemes and functors in the morphemes in the following utterances. Are there any kinds of lexemes which have functors inside them or attached to them and does this fact give any indication of how lexemes themselves might be classified into kinds?

(a) The outlook for the stock market seem-s to be better than many investor-s imagine. (b) The regular user-s of M1 are now old hand-s, and the road continue-s to be the saf-est in the country in relation to the volume of traffic it carri-es. (c) The number of neolithic site-s uncover-ed in the past thirteen year-s amount-s to over three hundred, of which more than one hundred are now excavate-d. (d) Even in limit-ed field-s of research, such as elementary particle physics or space investigation-s, expenditure on a single project may be so great as to make appreciable demand-s on the national exchequer, and so some degree of central control and foresight is require-d.

**2** If we compare the words *better* and *safest* we can find an odd but instructive discrepancy. From *safest* we can derive the word *safe* if we know such a paradigm as *simple, simpler, simplest*. And if the author of (a) above had written *brighter*, say, instead of *better*, we could have derived the word *bright* from the same or a similar paradigm. But we cannot derive the word *bet* (or *bett*—spelling is not usually a criterion of linguistic form) from *better*, because although we can find sentences containing the word *safe* or *bright* we cannot substitute the word *bet* (or *bett*) for *safe* or *bright*. Therefore we can say that *better* is a morpheme on its own, an exceptional one, although *safest* and *brighter* are two morphemes each.

Can you find similar examples?

**3** A variant of a word is a form of it. Thus any word in the paradigm *walk, walks, walking, walked* is a variant of any of the others. Such a series as this is called a **paradigm** because there are many other words with the same morphemes occurring at the ends of them. The morphemes -*s*, -*ing*, -*ed*, or the -*s* which denotes the plural as in *book / books*, are called inflexions. An **inflexion** is a bound morpheme which is formally contrastive. A **bound morpheme** is one which in the ordinary everyday use of the language does not exist by itself but is always joined to another morpheme which is also a lexeme, and the two together make another lexeme with a meaning different from the lexeme without the bound morpheme or with another bound morpheme. Thus *walks* and *walked* are both lexemes and both have different meanings.

Identify the bound morphemes or inflexions in the following sentences and find variants of the lexemes to which the morphemes are bound, and indicate the semantic and formal contrasts:

(a) Woollen fabrics in yellowish-brown shades are fashionable this winter. (b) When rainwater seeps into the soil, it absorbs organic matter. (c) The emigration of top-grade scientists from Britain is nothing new. (d) This latest film gives both these actors an opportunity of showing new aspects of their talents. (e) Vast quantities of decaying matter are carried by rivers.

# Chapter 13

# Immediate Constituents

In order to make sense in acts of communication, the words or morphemes of a language have to be arranged in patterns according to certain linguistic laws, which do, of course, arise by conventional use in everyday acts of communication that occur among the members of the speech-community. In the investigation of these laws by means of the analysis of thousands of utterances, linguists have found that such patterns are very often (though by no means always) made in pairs, and that sentences and the sub-structures that make sentences can be split successively into two parts, so that the whole shapes of sentences and the relationships of the segments in them can be revealed.

These parts are called by the general name of **Immediate Constituents**, usually abbreviated to ICs. Linguists have also invented a method of analysing structures to display what is called linear and hierarchical arrangements of any utterances in the language. This apparatus, which is absurdly simple to operate, merely splits utterances successively into their ICs in ranks, making one split per rank in any structure, starting with the larger ones and working down through the smaller to the smallest. Here is an example:

The    bowlers    of Sussex  had  their  moments.

| The | bowlers | of Sussex | had | their | moments. | | | 1 |
|-----|---------|-----------|-----|-------|----------|---|---|---|
| The | bowlers | of Sussex | had | their | moments. | | | 2 |
| The | bowlers | of Sussex | had | their | moments. | | | 3 |
| The | bowler | -s | of | Sussex | had | their | moment | -s. | 4 |

43

In each successive rank (the ranks are numbered on the right), one split is made in each segment. There can thus be two segments in the first rank, four in the second, eight in the third, and so on in geometric progression, though the actual number of segments in each rank will depend on the total number of morphemes in the utterance.

Another method of setting out the analysis could be like this?

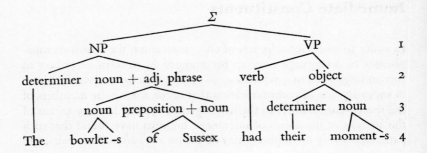

Here the Greek letter sigma, $\Sigma$, stands for Sentence, or the sum total of what is to be analysed, and the expressions NP and VP could stand for 'nominal part' and 'verbal part' respectively. In American usage NP and VP stand for 'noun phrase' and 'verb phrase', but it seems better to restrict the use of the word *phrase* for application to a common structure of 'preposition + nominal segment' (see page 55).

This sort of analysis is sometimes referred to as 'Phrase-Structure Grammar', and is the basis of finding out about the sentences of a language in order to construct a 'transformational grammar' or one that can generate other sentences.

## Exercises 13

**1** Look through some of the exercises given in this book and make IC analyses of some of the sentences, using both methods of setting out the analysis given on the previous two pages.

**2** One of the disadvantages of IC analysis, and its resolution of utterances into morphemes, is that it only works one way. We can only take existing sentences that have already been found in the actual use of the language and analyse them. But we cannot learn from IC analysis whether the sentences we take are grammatical ones (well-formed ones) or not, for there is always the possibility of some ambiguity in some English utterances. This means that some utterances can be analysed in two ways, both equally valid. Consider, for instance, the famous headline 'GIANT WAVES DOWN FUNNEL' over an article about a storm at sea; or consider the difference between the segments beginning with *by* in these sentences: 'The work was finished by nine o'clock' / 'The work was finished by his secretary'.

Even so, the fact that IC analysis can reveal the existence of such sentences as these shows that it can have some value in drawing our attention to the sorts of utterances that can occur in the language.

In what ways are the following utterances ambiguous? How can the ambiguity be resolved in spoken form and how in written form? Can IC analysis resolve the ambiguities? The utterances are printed here with the minimum of typographical support. (**Typographical support** is the help given, in graphic substance, by spelling, punctuation, layout, various kinds of type-face, underlining, and so on. With the spoken word, clear pronunciation, intonation, and even such extra-linguistic aids as facial expression, gesture, pointing, and so on, can help the speaker in making clear his meaning to his listener or listeners.)

(a) he was taken in by her assumed friendliness (b) he was taken in by the side door (c) ware is the town in hertfordshire (d) where is the town in hertfordshire (e) they were walking over the old bridge (f) they were talking over the old days (f) he was reading a book on the lawn (g) he was reading a book on the law of contract (h) charles stood firmly by amanda in her difficulties (j) charles stood firmly by the door of his office.

**3** Deal with the following utterances in the same way as those dealt with in the previous exercise:

(a) olympics television broadcast controversy (b) these stuffed shirts in the space age (c) british transports fly in milk and potatoes (d) john put that book down (e) government parties take back seats in italy (f) beat groups row over ferry crossing (g) taste this wine dont throw it away (h) rates tribunal talks hitch (i) crawley new town held up by lack of cement (j) precast concrete foreman wanted immediately (k) new city centre traffic lights probe findings (l) gilts again in the lead (m) general flies back to front (n) he was not available because he had gone to paris (o) in this light the article seems less difficult (p) she said she was one of the directors wives (q) global export figures tell very little about these changes influenced as they are by massive ups and downs in the export of primary products (r) a sound level meter consists essentially of a microphone amplifier weighting network and indicating instrument (s) savings and investments are not equal because the rate of interest operates to make them equal (t) the idea that every university must teach as far as possible every academic subject to be respectable has been abandoned.

# Chapter 14

## Grammaticality

What exactly is a grammatical utterance? As we saw in the previous section, some utterances can be analysed in at least two ways. If that is so, then either such utterances have some built-in ambiguity or such utterances are grammatical in one kind of use of the language but not in another. It is of course quite true to say that what is grammatical in one dialect of a language is not considered to be grammatical in a different dialect. Such a sentence as 'Our Mam done that' is quite grammatical within the dialect in which it exists, but some people would say that it was not 'good English' because it does not conform to the usages of the dialect in which 'My Mummy did that' is considered the normal sort of standard. In the same sort of way, many 'common errors' (as they are called in school textbooks of English composition) are just dialectal usages.

However, there are some points at which IC analysis fails. IC analysis could deal with such an utterance as 'Golf plays John' just as efficiently (or inefficiently) as it could deal with 'John plays golf', yet most English-speaking people would say that 'Golf plays John' is silly. Nevertheless, we must not be surprised by, or dismiss out of hand, those sentences which strike us as not conforming to the kinds of patterns we are used to. A sentence like 'Our Mam done that' is grammatical in its own dialect; and a sentence like 'A suspension of NO-dimethylaporotioraminol iodine (0.5g) in N-sodium hydroxide (50 ml) containing permanganate (1g) was shaken during 1 hr', taken from a respectable scientific journal, may be just as incomprehensible to some people as 'Golf plays John'.

Such thoughts as these lead us to the ideas, which we shall refer to later, of idiolect, dialect, register and style. Language is an activity, and it is an activity which takes place in circumstances and situations. For every occasion of language activity we can assume a set of circumstances which call forth that language activity. **Context** could be a name for such a set of circumstances. It is clear that context will have a great influence on the language activity it calls forth; it will influence what is said, its subject-matter, the vocabulary, the kind of sentences used to say it and so on. And since the speaker or writer will speak or write to or for somebody else in that context, the way in which he speaks or writes will be influenced by his audience or reader. Adults don't speak to small children in the same way as they speak to other adults. We don't write chemistry textbooks in the same way as we write love stories in women's magazines. Experts talking among themselves would not speak in the same way as when talking to laymen on the same topic. Different subject-matters dictate different ways of speaking and writing about them, and so on.

A sentence is grammatical if it conforms to the conventions of the kind of context that calls it forth. This means, of course, that a sentence which is grammatical in one set of relationships, or according to one idea of language use, may not be grammatical in another.

# Exercises 14

**1** Find or invent sentences containing the following words and show how the accentuation of them is contrastive grammatically:

absent, abstract, accent, alternate, attribute, august, combine, concert, conduct, contract, convict, desert, detail, envelope, export, frequent, interchange, invalid, object, minute, present, produce, prophesy, rebel, record, refuse, separate, subject, survey.

Consider the words in their phonic substance only without reference to typographical support they may show in the written medium.

**2** The American linguist Noam Chomsky has said, 'If we take "meaningfulness" or "significance" seriously I think we must admit that

I noticed a round square

or

Colourless green ideas sleep furiously

are thoroughly meaningless and non-significant, but it seems to me that, as a speaker of English, I should regard these in some way as "grammatical sentences", and it can certainly be argued that the establishment of their non-significance lies outside grammar.'

But consider the following: 'Not being familiar with American "city terminology", before writing this essay I rang up J. C. Catford to ask if there were any "squares" in New York as there are in some English cities. Without knowing the reason for my question his first reply was: "Well, there are round squares, called circles or circuses or something", showing that the collocation "round square" can occur in a completely meaningful and yet spontaneous manner in ordinary conversation.' (Dixon, Robert M. W., *Linguistic Science and Logic*)

Discuss these ideas.

**3** Standards of 'correct' grammar were established for English in the eighteenth century chiefly by three Scotsmen, George Campbell, Lord Kames and Hugh Blair, who lectured and wrote on literary criticism, English composition and rhetoric and who set up their standard by reference to the examples found in the works of such writers as Dryden, Addison, Swift, Pope and Johnson. It was these 'Scottish rhetoricians' who first set down such 'rules' as those about not putting prepositions at the end of sentences, about not starting a sentence with *but*, about not splitting infinitives, about the difference between *owing to* and *due to*, about 'unrelated participles', and about such utterances as 'Everyone should do his bit' being 'grammatically correct' while such an utterance as 'Everyone should do their bit' was regarded as 'bad grammar'. In the nineteenth century, when the need for mass literacy became urgent, such notions as these were repeated in books of English grammar and composition and they are still with us in the twentieth century, and can be found in such handbooks of 'correct writing' as Fowler's *Modern English Usage* or Eric Partridge's *Usage and Abusage* as well as in many school and college textbooks and the recommendations of the authorities of English language examinations.

Discuss the idea of a 'correct' standard of grammar and usage. Why should the language of the industrial, technological, democratic twentieth century conform to the standards of the agricultural and aristocratic eighteenth century? How far has the imposition of such standards through teaching and the needs of examinations imposed trivial and sterile ideas about grammar in people's minds? Hundreds of very good writers, from Shakespeare down to the present-day writers, have not obeyed the 'rules': should they have done so? On the other hand, there is a great deal of bad writing easily found in newspapers, magazines and periodicals that can be picked up today on any newsagent's stall: is this because the imposition of 'standards of correctness' has failed, and if so, why has it failed? Is the setting up of a standard verging on something like literary censorship and an interference with freedom of speech? And if a standard is to be set up, who is going to do it—academies such as those in France and Sweden, examiners of English at some sort of school-leaving examination, the British Standards Institution, who?

# Chapter 15

# Segmentation

Immediate constituent analysis can reveal not only the linear structure of sentences, but also the hierarchical arrangement or rank of segments within a structure. In addition to this, it becomes clear from the study of a large number of examples of IC analysis that segments can be found in different sentences to make similar patterns to those in other sentences. Thus, for the two sentences 'Thousands flocked to the market place' and 'He drove to the farm entrance', not only can the two segments *to the market place* and *to the farm entrance* be transposed from one sentence to the other, but on an IC analysis frame they make exactly the same pattern.

Such notions as these lead to the idea that there might be a limited number of set patterns into which the morphemes of utterances can be conventionally arranged. We have already seen that there is a limited number of arrangements of what we have called groups that can appear in sentences, and that they very often appear in the same order in sentences of the same type. Consequently we have here a method of examining segments of utterances and comparing them.

At the basis of this method is the idea that the larger segments, say those usually found in the first and second and sometimes the third ranks, are arrangements of morphemes whose order is more or less unchangeable functionally and stylistically, whereas in whole utterances there are large segments which can be moved about without much functional or stylistic harm. Thus, in the sentence 'Thousands flocked to the market place, the segments *thousands | flocked | to the market place* can be transposed so as to say 'To the market place flocked thousands' or 'To the market place thousands flocked', and the different orders of segments are not unintelligible. But within the segments themselves no transposition of morphemes is possible. One could not say '*sthousand edflock the to place market' and expect to be readily understood by native speakers of English.

It is useful to have some technical terms to deal with states of affairs of this nature. Some linguists have suggested, as a general term for dealing with parts of utterances in any language, the word **segment**. The larger segments have been called **macrosegments** and the smaller ones **microsegments**. These two words are not very pleasant aesthetically—perhaps **macrotom** and **microtom** would be better. However, these words are used to apply to any language whatever, but in English, and for English, we already have the traditional words **clause** and **phrase** for parts of sentences larger than a single morpheme, and we ourselves in this book have already used the word **group**, so we can use these words for the major structures that are found inside sentences in English.

The actual size of a segment will, of course, depend on its function within the sentence in which it occurs. Some groups, for instance, such as *thousands* or *he* above, will consist of only one word; some, like the verbal group *flocked to the market place* will consist of several words.

## Exercises 15

**1** If we look at the groups of these three sentences (a) 'The bowlers of Sussex had their moments', (b) 'Their moments of happiness are few' and (c) 'Those were their moments', we can see that the group *their moments* can occur either as subject, object or complement. But we can also see that this group cannot be an intransitive or transitive verb because it cannot be put intelligibly in any verbal position in a sentence, and it cannot be a passive verb because it does not include any of the morphemes *am / is / are / was / were / -ed / -en / -ne*, as in such passive verb groups as say *was elected, is spoken, are done*.

Examination of a large number of sentences which have groups in common leads us to the hypothesis that we might make a system of classification of lexemes and functors according to the kinds of groups in which they appear or do not appear, in other words, according to their position. We might find too that larger segments such as clauses and phrases could be dealt with in a similar way.

This hypothesis leads to the idea that there are four classes or kinds of linguistic function or behaviour. We can describe these functions or ways of behaving as either **nominal, adjectival, verbal** or **adverbial**. The best way to define nominal, adjectival, verbal or adverbial behaviour is by the formal characteristic of position and sometimes form of parts of sentences, and these have yet to be deduced. But this can be said generally: nominal and verbal parts of sentences can occur by themselves as groups or can function as heads of groups, while adjectival and adverbial parts or segments are likely to appear inside groups as adjuncts to heads, although there are one or two exceptions, since adjectival segments can appear by themselves as complement groups and adverbial segments can appear as sentence-adverbs.

Consider these four sentences:

'Thousands flocked to the market place', 'True Beaujolais is an exclusive wine', 'Two natives of Manchester became novelists', 'Three short 4B.A. bolts hold the gang capacitor'. In these four sentences the following are nominal segments: *thousands, true Beaujolais, an exclusive wine, two natives of Manchester, novelists, three short 4B.A. bolts, the gang capacitor*; inside them are the adjectival segments *true, an exclusive, two, of Manchester, three short 4B.A., the gang*; the following are verbal segments *flocked to the market place, became, is, hold*; and inside one of them is the adverbial segment *to the market place*.

Classify the segments in these sentences: (a) The couple have a fortnight's holiday. (b) The visitors were already making their way across the lawn. (c) The design of a tap is dictated by the mechanism inside it. (d) The floors were found covered with kitchen refuse. (e) Burnt patches where braziers had stood could still be clearly seen.

**2** The position of a segment in an utterance has a great deal of influence on its function. In such a sentence as 'He drove to the farm entrance', the phrase *to the farm entrance* is adverbial because its immediate constituent is the verb *drove*. But in such a sentence as 'The route to the farm entrance is marked on the map', the phrase *to the farm entrance* is adjectival because its immediate constituent is the nominal segment *the route*. Find and discuss other examples from your reading.

**3** It will be noted that in such phrases as *to the market place, of Sussex, of Manchester, across the lawn, by the mechanism inside it*, and so on there is a segment (*the market place, Sussex, Manchester*, etc.) which could be a nominal group (subject, complement, object) following a morpheme (*to, of, across, by,* etc.). If one of the functions of nominal segments, or one of the positions in which nominal segments can be found, is following such morphemes, then it can be said that we can recognize and identify a segment as nominal because it can follow such a morpheme. This is a formal characteristic of position of nominal segments. Altogether there are five grammatical positions of nominal segments in English. Can you say what they are?

# Chapter 16

# Nominal Segments (I): Position

The different segments found in sentences can be examined either from the point of view of their position or, once they have been isolated, from that of their structure. The property of appearing in certain positions is one of the formal characteristics of different kinds of segments and must be one of the criteria by which differences can be recognized.

In English there are five characteristic positions of nominal segments which have grammatical significance and which affect the formal structure of utterances. They are 1) as subjects of sentences, 2) as complements, 3) as objects, either direct or indirect, or they can occur inside groups 4) after kinds of morphemes called prepositions in the formation of adjectival or adverbial adjuncts (phrases), or as subjects, complements or objects of clauses, or 5) in apposition to other nominal segments.

We have already isolated and examined subjects, complements and objects from the point of view of their position, and noted that the normal distribution of these groups in sentences is a syntagmatic sequence of the actor-action type, so that subjects normally come first and complements and objects after verbal groups.

In questions the normal order of subject-verb-object or -complement may be altered. It could be verbal element + subject + verbal element + object ('Shall we have lunch?') or verbal group + subject + complement ('Is this book a whodunit?').

In commands there is no subject, but there may be an object or a complement ('Do it now', 'Be a man'). In some commands there may be a nominal segment—in the sense that it could be substituted for another nominal segment in a different structure—as for example in his mother's reputed advice to George III, 'George, be a king'. Here the nominal segment *George* is a linguistic device for ensuring that the demand is directed to the right quarter. Such a use as this is called a **vocative**.

In such a sentence as 'An Italian girl, Grazia Cisternino, has been refused a marriage licence because, according to official records, she is dead', the nominal segment *an Italian girl* is followed immediately by another nominal segment *Grazia Cisternino*. Either of these segments could serve as the subject of the sentence, because, semantically considered, each is a different name for the same person, and the second is here included in the subject group to identify more exactly the meaning of the first. When this sort of thing happens the second of the two nominal segments is said to be in **apposition** to the first. Sometimes there is discontinuity in apposition, as in the sentence 'They don't know what they're doing, these so-called experts', where the nominal segment *these so-called experts* is in apposition to *they*.

## Exercises 16

1 Consider the nominal segments in the following sentences. Classify them according to position. Do any of them have structural properties which might suggest a different classification?

(a) Two big chemical companies yesterday reported a merry rise in profits. (b) A flicker of white through the trees distracted her. (c) The allocation of the quota will be based on brewers' import requirements as notified by them to the Permanent Joint Hops Committee. (d) Allegory seems somehow alien to the English temper. (e) All Commonwealth countries rely on the export of primary products—foodstuffs and minerals—for most of their foreign currency.

2 What do the italicized nominal segments in the following sentences have in common?

(a) *That modern furniture design is becoming increasingly honest and functional* is something to be applauded. (b) I asked myself *how much good had been done*. (c) *What is of great interest in this connexion* is the method of construction. (d) His answer was *that he knew nothing of the matter*. (e) The fact *that he said he had been there* was not considered proof *that he actually had*.

The nominal segments indicated in the first four of the sentences above are all clauses, in this case nominal or noun clauses. A **clause** is a sentence-like structure which nevertheless functions either as a group or inside a group. Nominal clauses can be groups in their own right as in sentences (a), (b), (c) and (d) above. In the fifth sentence the nominal clauses are co-ordinated in apposition to other nominal segments. The clause *that he said he had been there* is in apposition to the segment *the fact*, and *that he actually had* is in apposition to *proof*. Note that the clause *that he said he had been there* also contains a nominal clause *he had been there* inside it.

**3** Consider the following sentences in pairs. What does the subject of the first sentence of each pair have in common with the object of the second sentence of each pair?

(a) Trees which are native to higher latitudes have a short growing period in this country. The film ably showed the difficulties which the explorers encountered. (b) The three control panels, which are bolted to a permanent base, can be removed for inspection or maintenance. Lemon juice has many other uses which the housewife can soon discover. (c) The proposals that were submitted to the Ministry last week are now known to foreshadow drastic changes in the management of the aircraft industry. The Conservative Party, too, has had a successful record of which it can be proud.

A segment like *which are native to higher latitudes* is a clause because it has sentence-like structure (subject *which*; intransitive verb, *are*; complement, *native to higher latitudes*), and because it is also part of the group *trees which are native to higher latitudes* which is the subject of the first pair in (a). All the clauses of this exercise are adjectival clauses because they function as adjuncts to nominal segments or the heads of nominal groups. Adjectival clauses are not, like some nominal clauses, co-ordinated, but subordinated, and a sign of subordination is the presence in many of them of words like *who, whom, whose, which, that*, normally as an introductory functor.

**4** Discuss the complement groups in the following sentences and try to decide whether all of them can reasonably be called 'nominal segments' or not. If not, which complements deserve a different classification and why?

(a) Overnight she became famous. (b) The decision was not easy to take. (c) Tomorrow he will be twenty-one. (d) Other marks on the cattle are protective talismans, intended to ward off evil spirits. (e) Some lakes are too deep for plants to grow in the middle of them. (f) How you spend your money is your own affair. (g) The idea seemed to fascinate him. (h) Black paint is cheap. (i) His paintings are alive. (j) The film was a very old one.

# Chapter 17

# Nominal Segments (II): Structure

A very large number of English nominal segments (though not all) are composed of either heads and adjuncts or just heads by themselves. The rest are nominal clauses whose structure is like that of sentences. Looking at the sentences quoted in the exercises in this book, and ignoring those which contain nominal clauses, we can find the following sorts of examples of nominal segments:

1) Margot, she, he, they, him, this, I, thousands, allegory;
2) the inspector, this article, a vicar, their team, her head;
3) black paint, farm workers, fifty years, modern science, lemon juice;
4) their new car, the new ship, a fortnight's holiday, an exclusive wine, this latest film;
5) a model without electronic phasing; the Queen of Egypt; the outlook for the stock market; woollen fabrics in yellowish-brown shades;
6) a photo-electric cell connected to a galvanometer; the fears expressed by the Labour Party about reinvestment in electricity undertakings;
7) to go to arbitration; to be better than many investors imagine; to have plaster gnomes in their front gardens; to believe otherwise;
8) how to make your talents pay.

Certain facts stand out clearly. For instance, words like *the, a, this, their* do not appear in the first and third sections, and the words which follow such words as *the, a, this, their* in the fourth section do not allow themselves to be substituted for the words of the first section. Words like *of, for, without* clearly make adjectival phrases which appear in the fifth section, and in the sixth words ending in -*ed* seem to be important, while in the seventh the word *to* appears to play an important part.

The patient examination of features such as these will eventually

reveal systematic methods of patterning of particular kinds of morphemes. For instance, in those cases where nominal segments are simply
heads the morphemes which make the heads seem to fall into two main
kinds, those with words like *Margot, thousands* and *allegory,* and those
with words like *she, he, they, him.* Words of the second kind can correlate with those of the first kind in certain positions, but they never
seem to appear preceded by words like those of the first of each pair in
the third section. The words that appear in the second, third and fourth
sections also exhibit properties which seem to make them classifiable
in one way or another. A statistical analysis would show that *the / a / an /
this / that,* etc. occur with greater frequency than *latest / exclusive /
electronic / woollen,* etc. Moreover, these latter words seem to have
formal characteristics, such as the endings *-est, -ive, -ic, -en,* and the
possibility of being adjuncts, and some of them seem connected with
such words as *exclusion, electronics, wool,* which can be heads of nominal
segments but not always adjuncts.

We can see here the germ of the idea of **form-classes** or the possibility of describing different sorts of words or linguistic forms according
to differences of function known by means of differences of position
and form.

## Exercises 17

1 If we have a question like 'Did Margot tell the inspector what she
had done?' an answer to it like 'Yes, Margot did that' is clearly an
intelligible one. But the same answer could be just as intelligible to a
quite different question, such as 'Did Margot put the butter in the
fridge?' or 'Did Margot marry Ian after all?' Consequently, we can
say that the words *did that* could stand for, or symbolize, almost any
activity whatsoever, and almost any nominal segment could stand in
front of them as a subject—the only exceptions are words like *me, him,
her, us, them, whom,* etc. With this idea in mind we could construct a
**test-frame** to examine a large number of nominal segments. We simply
make IC analyses of a large number of sentences with any subject we
choose and with *did that* as transitive verb and object.

What words in the following list cannot produce intelligible results
on such a test-frame?

conventional, model, waiting, Sunday, him, many, they, his, who, like, profits, national, so, myself, from, space, changes, nothing, fortnight's, industry, something, known, required.

Invent, or find examples of, sentences containing words from the list which cannot make intelligible subjects, and discover in what kinds of positions they can occur.

**2** Examine the following segments on the test-frame:

black paint; fifty years; Congressional ratification; liquid hydrogen; their new car; an exclusive wine; this latest film; the new ship; a fortnight's holiday.

What do you notice about the rank of such morphemes as *their, the, a, an, this*? Try the effect on the test-frame of these words before each of the first four of the nominal segments given above (e.g., *this black paint*, so as to particularize the reference of the segment). What effect does this have on the rank of such words as *black, fifty*, etc.?

Is there anything different in the words *fortnight's* and *latest* which distinguishes them from such words as *black* and *new*?

**3** Discuss some of the problems which might arise in the analysis of these nominal segments considered as subjects on the test-frame:

a more basic question; two big chemical companies; his pretty blonde wife; the fat major's wife; crude, amateurish treatments; crudely amateurish treatments; three short 4B.A. bolts; elementary particle physics; guaranteed used cars.

What is the effect in these segments of the preceding words on the rank of the last word?

**4** Analyse the following segments on the test-frame:

a model without electronic phasing; the outlook for the stock market; the design of a tap; Bach at his warmest and most appealing; woollen fabrics in yellowish-brown shades; the fears expressed by the Labour Party about re-investment in electricity undertakings; the number of neolithic sites uncovered in the past thirteen years.

Distinguish between the functors and lexemes in the segments given above, and state what you notice about the relative ranks of each. What do you notice about the ranks of such morphemes as *without, for, of, at, in*, etc., in the phrases in which they occur?

# Chapter 18

# Form-classes (I)

Analysis of nominal segments shows that inside many of them there are several different kinds of smaller segments. We have now to try to discover some method of finding out how many different kinds of the smallest segments there are and what are our criteria for deciding how many and what the kinds are?

Whereas such words as *Margot, she, thousands, allegory* can function by themselves as nominal segments, there are other words, such as *the, a, an, their,* apparently making one kind, and *black, fifty, exclusive,* apparently making another, which can only function normally in combination with other words. Even so, English being what it is, there are some borderline cases, as in the sentences 'Black is an uninspiring colour' or 'Fifty is a larger number than ten'. Nevertheless, apart from the meanings of words (not always a reliable criterion), there are formal characteristics of position and sometimes of the possession of some such common ending as *-tion, -al, -ive,* which can help us to classify into various kinds the forms that make up segments.

By means of the technique of substitution in IC analysis test-frames we have already isolated two types of forms—such words as *Margot, thousands, allegory,* and such forms as *I, he, we, they,* etc., which can also form nominal segments (or fill the position of nominal segments) by themselves, but which are restricted in their ability to do so by the fact that some of them can only appear as subjects and some only as objects. By the same method we can also isolate such words as *the, a, an, this, their,* etc, and such words as *black, fifty, woollen, exclusive,* etc. We have also seen that some of the postmodifying adjuncts of heads in nominal segments are structures introduced by such words as *to, of, from, without, by,* etc. Thus we have isolated five different classes of words.

To members of the first class (*Margot, allegory,* etc.) the name noun is traditionally given, and we might define the word **noun** as meaning a lexeme which can function typically as the head of a nominal segment.

To members of the second class (*I*, *me*, etc.) the name pronoun is traditionally given, and we might define the word **pronoun** as meaning a functor which can correlate with a noun or a nominal segment or group.

To members of the third class (*the*, *a*, *an*, etc.) traditional grammar has given no consistent nomenclature, but modern linguistics gives to them the name **determiner**, which we may define as meaning a functor which as a premodifying adjunct shows its head to be a noun.

To members of the fourth kind (*exclusive*, *woollen*, etc.), the name traditionally given is **adjective**, which we might define as meaning a lexeme which functions typically as an adjunct premodifying a noun and sometimes as the head of a complement group.

To members of the fifth kind (*to*, *for*, *by*, etc.) the name traditionally given is **preposition**, which we might define as meaning a functor which precedes a nominal segment in the formation of an adjectival or adverbial phrase.

## Exercises 18

1 'A noun is the name of a person, place or thing.' 'An adjective is a describing word.' Compare these definitions, taken from school textbooks on English grammar, with those given on above. Discuss the differences.

2 From a comparison of a number of nominal segments taken from books, magazines and newspapers, see whether you can systematically describe the class of words called nouns. Why do some nouns need determiners before them and some not? Which sorts do and which don't? Is it possible to evolve a set of rules, which would be helpful to a foreigner learning English, about the relationships between determiners and nouns?

3 By means of IC analysis or otherwise check and report on the validity of this statement: 'Names like George, Margaret, Edinburgh or Mars, which particularize with unambiguous definiteness, are normally of

higher rank in utterances than the so-called common nouns, which are names shared by a large number of things.' Explain why the two adjectival clauses in this statement could be linguistically irrelevant.

**4** Collect examples of nominal segments which contain determiners. What are the considerations that might lead one to suppose that the determiners of English form a system?

The following is a list of some of the determiners of English: *a, an, any, all, either, neither, few, every, some, no, half, the, this, that, these, those, such, my, his, its, her, our, your, their*, and the cardinal numbers *one, two* to *ninety-nine*.
Discover and list others.

In what ways do determiners like, *my, his, her, its, our, your, their* or like *this, that, these, those* show special characteristics of their own?

**5** 'An adjective is a lexeme which functions typically as an adjunct premodifying a noun.' Yet adjectival phrases and clauses typically postmodify or come after nouns. Why?

Can you find examples of adjectives which come after nouns? How can you account for this apparent discrepancy?
Find examples of strings of adjectives before nouns, as in 'three short 4B.A. bolts'. Is there any principle that you can discover which decides the order in which the adjectives should occur?

**6** Language economy sometimes makes forms do double duty, so that we can say, for instance, 'I like these better than (I like) those', where the context, or situation in which the utterance occurs, makes clear the referential meaning of *these* and *those*.

Collect examples of transposition, as it is called, or one form-class exponent turning up in a place where one would expect a word of a different form-class.

The word *population*, for instance, is most often likely to be found in nominal positions, but in such an expression as *the population problems of Asia* it is in an adjectival position and its behaviour is adjectival. In the sentence 'There is a green hill far away', the word *there* is in a nominal position as subject: is it therefore a noun?

How would you classify the italicized words in 'This is *mine | his | hers | its | ours | yours | theirs*?

# Chapter 19

# Verbal Segments

Considered from the point of view of position, verbal segments are absurdly simple. Their only characteristic position as groups is after the subject or before the complement or object. But considered from the point of view of structure, verbal segments are more complex.

The first thing to do in considering verbal segments is to separate heads from adjuncts. In such a sentence as 'Thousands flocked to the market place', the phrase *to the market place* can have substituted for it such words as *yesterday, eagerly, quickly,* and we can easily find such verbal groups as *were already making* where *already* can be replaced by a large number of words many of which end with *-ly*. We can thus isolate a class of words of adverbial function which we can call adverbs, and the word **adverb** can be defined as meaning a lexeme functioning typically as the adjunct of a verb, or as an adjunct to an adjective or another adverb (for we can find such expressions as 'an *easily* distinguishable phenomenon' or '*very* readily given help').

We have already characterized verbal segments as groups which can be intransitive, transitive or passive. Verbal segments take on these characteristics from their heads, which are of course verbs. Verbal forms belong to three main kinds, two classes of lexemes and a system of functors. We can define a **finite verb** as a lexeme which functions typically as the head of a verbal segment. We can define an **infinitive verb** as a lexeme which consists either of the base of the verb or the base of the verb with the addition of one of the morphemes *to, -ing, -ed* or an allomorph of the last. (The **base** of a verb can be said to be the dictionary form of it, e.g., *walk, be, have, sing, speak.* An **allomorph** is a morpheme of the same class or system which has the same function as another morpheme of a different form: thus, the speech-sounds /s, z, ɪz/ as they are heard at the ends of the words *walks/tries/sneezes/* are allomorphs of one another.) The third type of verb forms we may call **operators.** The word *operator* can be defined as meaning a functor which occurs typically before infinitive verbs to indicate variations of mood or tense. Examples are such words as *am/is/are/was/were/been/ being/has/have/had/do/does/did/will/would/shall/should/can/could/may/might /must/ought*.

# Exercises 19

**1** In English the verbs *to be* and *to have* can function both as lexemes and functors. In such SIC sentences as 'Swallows are insect-eating birds' or 'London is a city', the forms *are* and *is* are lexemes; and in such STO sentences as 'She has fair hair' or 'He had lunch in New York', the forms *has* and *had* are also lexemes. But forms of the verb *to be* coming before other verb forms ending in *-ing*, or forms of the verb *to have* coming before other verb forms ending in *-ed* (or one of its allomorphs) are functors. Thus in the sentences 'Swallows are flying low' and 'He has finished lunch' *are* and *has* are functors.

Collect examples of sentences with *am/is/are/was/were* occurring before verb forms ending in *-ing*, and examples of *have/has/had* occurring before verb forms ending in *-ed*, *-en* or words like *sung, done, made*, etc. Can you explain the function of these functors?

**2** Some adjuncts of verbal groups are phrases and some are adverbial clauses. Consider the following:

He waited until she was ready / He waited until noon. He telephoned me after I had left / I entered after him. He stood before the altar / I left before I could see him.

What justification is there for supposing that the words *until, after* and *before* can belong to two different form-classes?

**3** In such a sentence as 'Yesterday he drove to the farm entrance' the form *to* is a preposition before a nominal segment making an adverbial phrase. Do the italicized forms in the following sentences have the same function or a different one? If it is different can you explain what the difference is?

(a) The Prime Minister hit *back* at his opponents. (b) Japan frowns *on* tipping. (c) Britain relies *on* exports. (d) We don't know what goes *on* in other people's minds. (e) Carry *on* with your work. (f) After the quarrel they made it *up*. (g) When it fell, he picked it *up*. (h) School breaks *up*. (i) He made *up* the whole story. (j) The car broke *down*.

**4** Verbs such as those exemplified above (*to break down*) are called **phrasal verbs,** because the verb base is modified in some way by the addition of an item that is neither an adverb nor a preposition, but simply a morpheme that has the same kind of effect as a suffix. Explain the differences in the verb forms in the following pairs of sentences:

I came across an old friend in Oxford last week / I came across the fields on the way home. You turn off the main road just past the King's Head / Turn off the light. She put on her new dress / You can put on a person like that. He ran through the items on the list / He ran through the bushes.

**5** Look through the sentences given in the exercises in this book and find examples which have sentence-adverbs—'Yesterday he drove to the farm entrance.' Try the experiment of putting the sentence-adverbs as adjunct pre- and post-modifying the head of the verbal group. What effect does this have on the rank of other items in the sentences? What effect does it have on meaning?

**6** The items italicized in the following sentences are operators. Describe their function. Make IC analyses of the sentences and note the rank of operators and their effect on the rank of other items in verbal segments. (a) I like Brahms—*do* you like Brahms? (b) We *must* all pull together. (c) I *may* come to see you next week. (d) We *can* do it, of course, but I *do* not think we *should* do it just yet. (e) We *cannot* do it, and I *do* not think we *should* try. (f) I *would* like to see you, but I *shall* be away when you *can* come to Paris. (g) He *might* arrive this evening. (h) He *might have* arrived yesterday. (i) I *am being* interviewed by the Board to-morrow, and *could* not leave until afterwards. (j) He *has* not *been* known to fail.

If *cannot, can't* and possibly *don't, doesn't, didn't* can be called operators, how does one deal with *not* as in, say, (d) above?

# Chapter 20

# Form-classes (II)

We have so far isolated eight different kinds of morphemes—nouns, adjectives, verbs and adverbs (these make four classes of lexemes), and determiners, pronouns, prepositions and operators (these make four systems of functors. Altogether there are fourteen different kinds of morphemes in English. There are the four kinds of lexemes we have already isolated which form a great class of words or morphemes and to which new items in the language may be added at any time. And there are ten systems of functors, four of which we already know. There are, therefore, six more systems of functors to be accounted for.

Linguistic forms in English may be joined together. We can have a structure like 'bread and butter' where two nouns are joined by *and*, or like 'He is slow but painstaking' where two adjectives are joined by *but*, or two sentences can be joined together as in the sentence quoted in the first paragraph of Chapter 6. Such words as *and/but/so/or*, and their allied forms in function, the disjunctive *either . . . or / neither . . . nor* are called **conjunctions**, which may be defined as functors which co-ordinate structures or forms of equal rank.

Clauses, as we have seen, have properties which make them sentence-like, but all clauses occur inside other sentences and all except nominal clauses occur either as adjuncts or sentence-adverbs. All clauses can be, and most are, joined to the rest of the structure in which they belong by such words as *that/which/who/when/where/if/unless/because/although*, etc., which we can call **subordinators**, which may be defined as functors behaving typically as link-morphemes between clauses and the rest of the structure to which they belong.

There are some words like *why/how/when/where/what/whence/whither/whether*, along with *who/whom/whose/which* that can appear either at the beginnings of nominal clauses or at the beginnings of questions. We may call these **interrogatives**, which we can define as functors which function typically as signallers of question-form.

Since they are functionally contrastive, some forms which exist as inflexions must also be included in the catalogue of English morphemes. In this way we must count **verb inflexions**, such as *-s/-es/-ing/to and-ed* and its allomorphs and can define them as functors which behave morphologically to signal different functions of verb bases. In a similar kind of way there are a number of other inflexional morphemes. Those which signal the plural form of nouns, for instance, *-s* and its allomorphs of various sorts (*cat/cats, box/boxes, foot/feet, formula/formulae,* and so on), must be counted as belonging to a system. We may define these **noun inflexions** as functors which signal plurality when added to singular forms. Also there are the adjectival and adverbial inflexions *-er/-est*, which we may call **comparatives**, which signal degrees of comparison or itensity of difference of adjectives or adverbs. The allomorphs of these comparatives, *more* and *most*, can also be included here.

# Exercises 20

**1** Using such criteria of position as have been indicated in previous chapters, explain the function of the italicized forms in the following and assign to form-classes:

(a) At *last*, in the 10th century AD, the Chinese governor was driven *out* of the province, *and* a patriot proclaimed himself the first governor of Vietnam. (b) Whether it will be a *Government* body, an independent body, *or* a body *representative* of the Government, employers and unions, was left *unsettled*. (c) Their troughs are raised *off* the ground, *so* the pigs have *to stretch* on their hind legs *to eat*. (d) The two controls are *so* clearly marked that you can see at a glance *how* to set them, but so *very* cold weather quicker *warming up* would make passengers *more* comfortable. (e) He was *so* clever he could do it *himself*. (f) He was so clever that he could do it by *himself*. (g) This morning he cut *himself while* shaving. (h) I like *myself* more than I like anybody *else*. (i) They were not allowed to do it by *themselves*. (j) You had *better not* do that or *else* you might hurt *yourself*.

**2** Consider and discuss the following questions:

1) What is the difference in function in the following italicized

examples? '*That* is right' / 'He said *that* it was right' / '*That* what he said was right is well known' / 'This is the one *that* is right'.

2) What is the difference in function in the following italicized examples? '*What* time is it?' / '*What* is the time?' / 'I know *what* I like' / '*What* a lot of fuss about nothing'.

3) Is the function of *who* the same in 'I know who did it' as in 'Who did it?'?

4) Is there any point in making a distinction of form-class in morphemes like *who/whom/whose/which* and sometimes *that* when they come at the beginnings of adjectival clauses and at the beginnings of nominal clauses? In the sentences 'He said that he was going to America' and 'He told us who did it' what is the real difference between *that* and *who*?

5) In such a structure as 'Who told you?' the form *who* clearly has some function as a signaller of question-form since 'He told you' is not necessarily a question. Is *who* partly a signaller of question-form in 'He asked who did it' and in 'He told us who did it' or not? Is the distinction between subordinators and interrogatives a significant one?

6) Consider the function of intonation in the spoken form of questions. Use a tape-recorder to collect examples of yourself and your colleagues asking questions with various intonations, and note differences and similarities.

**3** Can you draw up a set of rules for the use of *that* in its various functions, so as to enable a foreigner learning English to speak and write it idiomatically?

**4** Write a short clear explanation, suitable for a foreigner learning English, of the use of comparatives, the system of the functors *-er*, *-est*, *more*, *most*. Why should he say *small, smaller, smallest*, but not *wonderful, *wonderfuller, *wonderfullest*? Are there any irregular forms of comparison other than *good, better, best*? How would you explain the difference between the *-er* of *bigger* and the *-er* of *driver*?

# Chapter 21

# Morphology (I)

**Morphology** is the study of the behaviour of linguistic units called morphemes. This perfectly general definition can apply to all languages. But so far as English is concerned the chief characteristics of the changes that morphemes undergo is that they are consistent. The changes are confined mainly to classes of forms and concern noun inflexions, verb inflexions and comparatives. Pronouns and those subordinators which have pronominal properties (*who/whom*, for instance) are the only members of systems which show morphological changes. The morphological systems are sometimes referred to as 'grammatical categories', and so far as Present-day English is concerned these deal with 1) the number system of nouns, 2) the case systems of pronouns, 3) the comparison system of adjectives and adverbs, and 4) the various grammatical systems of verb forms.

**Number** is a linguistic technical term used to describe a system of special forms which indicate whether one or more than one is spoken about. In Present-day English a distinction is usually made between singular and plural, and generally the distinction is shown by means of the absence or presence of a suffix (*cow/cows, box/boxes, child/children, nebula/nebulae*) or by membership of a system of forms in which the internal vowel is replaced (*mouse/mice, man/men, foot/feet*). By far the largest number of English nouns form their plurals by the addition of a variety of sibilants represented in writing by -*s* or -*es*.

There is a form of patterning, or **colligation**, by which certain determiners support the morphological forms indicated above. Determiners like *a/an/every/each/this/that* always colligate with singular forms, and determiners like *these/those/all/many/some*, etc. always colligate with plurals.

**Case** is a linguistic technical term to describe a variation in form which indicates syntactic relations with other forms in an utterance. In Present-day English only pronouns can be said to show case, as in the

73

pairs *I/me, he/him, she/her*, etc., where the first member of each pair can correlate with subjects and the second can correlate with objects or follow prepositions. In Old English both nouns and adjectives as well as pronouns showed variations of case, but the only survivor nowadays of any of these variants is the morpheme *-'s/-s* as in *John's books, some photographers' cameras*. In all positions where this form occurs nowadays its function is precisely like that of an adjective.

**Comparison** is a linguistic term for forms which show degrees of intensity of difference. English has positive (base form of an adjective or adverb), comparative (*-er, more*), and superlative (*-est, most*). The comparative is often used with the subordinator *than* before adjectival clauses, as in 'He is taller than his brother (is)' or 'He works more industriously than his brother (does)'. The positive form of adjectives or adverbs is used with the compound subordinator *as . . . as* to denote equality of comparison (or with the adverb *not* to denote inequality), as in 'He is as tall as his brother (is)' or 'A dollar is not worth as much as a pound (is)'.

# Exercises 21

1 The 'normal' morphological change that forms the plurals of nouns in Present-day English is the addition of the morpheme /s/ or /z/ or /iz/ (represented in writing by *-s/-es*) to the singular form.

What are the circumstances that dictate the phonological forms of the allomorphs used in Present-day English pronunciation to form plurals.

What phonological or phonemic changes are influenced by the singulars that follow in the formation of the plural? church, edge, boy, noise, cup, princess, sneeze, bath, calf, hoof, roof, youth, wreath, judge.

2 Classify the following nouns according to the morphological changes found in the formation of their plurals. Comment on oddities or exceptions. Do any belong to systems?

child, crew, blacksmith, genus, protectorate, alms, criterion, woman, shelf, crisis, fish, virtuoso, penny, die, datum, fungus, mother-in-law, genius, sheep, house, brother, cherub.

**3** Consider the indicated plurals in the following utterances. What sort of linguistic description would you give of them?

(a) She owes her success to her good *looks*. (b) *Eland* are nearly extinct in this part of Africa. (c) I am no longer *friends* with you. (d) They went for a walk across the *sands*. (e) He gazed up into the *heavens*. (f) If you go down in the *woods* today prepare for a big surprise. (g) I've not done it yet, but I live in *hopes*.

**4** What is linguistically significant or unusual about the following words and their relationship with number?

statistics, physics, pence, annals, trousers, game, measles, oats, Japanese, species, deer, hangers-on, spoonful, information, billiards, truth, beauty, goodness, classics, bureau, glass, clergy, knowledge, police, cattle, the Joneses, antipodes, scissors, phonetics.

**5** What is your opinion about such questions as the colligation of nouns with verb forms in such uses as 'The committee have agreed . . .' or 'The committee has agreed . . .' or 'The Government is considering . . .' or 'The Government are considering . . .'?

How can one decide how the singularity or plurality of such words as *committee, government, team, crew, crowd, flock, congregation*, etc., should be determined? Is it a question for individual speakers and writers, linguists, or whom?

**6** The technical terms **reflexive** and **intensifier** are used for pronominal forms ending in *-self*, plural *-selves*. 'He cut himself while shaving' illustrates the first, and 'He actually did it himself' illustrates the second. Find and discuss other examples and possible ambiguities.

# Chapter 22

# Morphology (II)

Since the verbal groups in sentences play such a dominating part, we might expect that the morphology of the verb-forms of the language is more complicated than that of other form-classes, and this is certainly so. Indeed, with regard to the verbal system of English the term *form-class* can be misleading, since forms that appear from one point of view to be verb-like may from another point of view appear to be different and may belong to more than one form-class at the same time.

There is not space here to account completely for the whole of the morphology of English verb-forms. But the reader should note first the paradigms of the so-called weak verbs—those which form their past tense by the addition of the morpheme *-ed*—and of the so-called strong or vocalic verbs—those which form their past tense by the replacement of the vowel of the base (as with *speak/spoke* or *swim/swam*).

The reader should also note that verb-forms can have the properties of person, number, mood, voice and tense, and they can also have the property of finitude.

The best way of proceeding is to collect examples of utterances and to isolate those verbal forms which can be classified according to these categories.

**Person** is that property by which some forms will colligate only with certain pronouns or pronoun substitutes, as *am* will colligate only with *I*. **Number** is the property of some verb-forms to colligate only with singular subjects and others only with plural subjects, as in *he speaks/they speak* or *he is/we are*. **Mood** is a kind of anomalous form which signals some kind of semantic difference, as in 'If I were you . . .', where *were*, which does not normally colligate with *I*, shows a hypothesis of unlikely fulfilment; or mood can show a structural difference of sentence-form, as in the **indicative mood** of 'I stand at ease' and in the **imperative mood** of 'Stand at ease'. **Voice** is a form of verb patterning which indicates the relationship of verb to subject; in English there is the **active voice**, where the subject is related to the action of the verb in the relationship of actor-action, and there is the **passive voice** where the form is indicated by a past participle following a finite form of the verb *to be*. **Tense** is a form of the verb which expresses the idea of time of action in relation to the time of utterance.

Verb-forms also have a property called **finitude**; they can be **finite** if they can follow in use one or another of the pronouns *I/he/she/we/ you/they*. All those preceded by the morpheme *to*, many base forms preceded by such operators as *will/would/shall/should/may/might*, etc., some ending with *-ed*, many ending with *-en* (*frozen, been*), many with replaced vowels different from their present and past finite form (*begun, sung*), and all ending with *-ing* are **non-finite** or **infinitive**.

Infinitives can have a double function. *To*+base (the **infinitive**) can have a variety of double functions according to position. Base+*ing* (the **gerund**) can be both nominal and verbal. Base+*ed* or allomorph (**past participle**) and base+ing (**present participle**) can be either verbal and adjectival or, sometimes, verbal and adverbial.

# Exercises 22

**1** Some grammarians divide the English verbs into two categories, a system of verbs which they call **strong** or **vocalic**, which are distinguished by their forming their past tense by replacing the vowel of the base (*sing/sang, break/broke, blow/blew*), and a class of verbs called **weak**, which are distinguished by their forming their past tense by the addition of *-ed* to the base (*walk/walked, admire/admired, criticize/criticized*).

Make lists of examples of both types and discuss their grammatical and semantic differences.

Into which categories would you put the following verbs and why?

contemplate, awake, awaken, dream, have, think, do, buy, understand, make, say, go, cut, establish, inform, pasteurize, hesitate, put, cut.

Into which categories would you put the irregular verbs of the language, and which categories would you expect to find them in and why?

Into which categories would new verbs added to the language be likely to be put and why?

**2** The infinitive *to*+base has a variety of functions. By means of positional criteria determine the function of the italicized infinitives in the following sentences:

(a) He wanted *to go*. (b) *To believe* otherwise would be foolish. (c) We waited for the messenger *to arrive*. (d) Stop *to think* what you are going *to do*. (e) Business men are likely *to remain* sceptical about the proposals *to control* prices. (f) They know what *to expect*. (g) He was not ready *to pay* the price asked. (h) They were just about *to begin* their meal when the telephone began *to ring* in the next flat. (i) He went there *to see* what had happened. (j) He spoke slowly so as *to make* his meaning clearer.

Add to these examples from your own reading. Find examples of the base used as an infinitive as in 'Let's go'.

**3** Distinguish among, and discuss the function of, the indicated gerunds and past participles in the following sentences:

(a) The plan *suggested* has been *turned down*. (b) *Sitting* in the restaurant, she saw him enter and guessed his *coming* was fortuitous. (c) *Surprised* by this remark, Simon was *tempted* to think she had been *told* about the journey. (d) Without *thinking*, he had *turned* and *seen* it. (e) He was not then ready to pay the price *asked*. (f) They did not like his *being* there. (g) In *attempting* to assess the value of these two differing views, we must not be *blinded* by prejudice against what has *happened* in the past or pleasure in *sensing* what is going to happen in the future.

**4** The system of verbal functors we have called operators consists of the items listed on page 68.

Collect examples from your reading of operators in use. Consider and discuss the use of operators with present and past participles and bases in the formation of tenses, passive verb groups, mood.

In what circumstances can operators be lexemes and not functors?

Why are the forms *having, doing, done* not on the list?

What is the function of operators in questions?

**5** 'We can ask him when he comes tomorrow.' 'I am going to London on Tuesday.'

Old English had no future tense forms. Using the two sentences above and others like them of your own finding, discuss the use of adverbs or adverb phrases in the indication of time-relationships, when the form of the verb seems not to indicate them.

'The radii of a circle are all equal.' In what way does the tense-indication in this sentence differ from that in the sentence used by a television cookery expert: 'I cream the butter and then I add the sugar'?

'He tells me you've bought a new car.' When did he do the telling?

Discuss these and other examples which you can find of time-relationships expressed by English tense-forms.

# Chapter 23

# Lexis

Lexis is that part of linguistics which deals with the main units of language that carry the main burden of referential meaning.

The idea of morphology naturally leads to what might be called the **paradigmatic relations** of words. A **paradigm** is a linguistic model, as in the list *distribute/distribution/distributive/distributory*, where the suffixes are signs of possible different form-classes not only of the words in the list but of other words with similar endings, so that if we know, say, *contribute*, we can deduce the existence of *contribution/ contributive/contributory*. In some paradigms we can have different kinds of words in the same form-class, as in, say, *critic/critical/critically/ criticism*, where *critic* and *criticism* are both nouns not semantically interchangeable, and where *critical* can have more than one meaning according to the register in which it is used.

Words can also have **syntagmatic relations**, that is, words which can have separate individual existence often appear with others in tight or loose associations. A tight association is seen in the making of **compounds**, where two separate morphemes join together to form a new morpheme, as in the word *blackbird*. Looser associations are seen in what are known as **collocations**, conventional associations of particular words together in sentences or parts of sentences. Thus, we can speak of an *old-age pensioner* and *old-time dancing*, but not of an *old-time pensioner* or *old-age dancing*. Some words seem to occur only in collocations, for instance, *maiden* is rarely used nowadays to mean 'girl', but appears in such collocations as *maiden voyage/maiden speech/ maiden over* (in cricket)/*maiden aunt*. A particular form of collocation is a **cliché**, a collocation so well used it has become almost meaningless, as *seldom if ever* or *this day and age*. **Idioms**, too, are collocations whose meanings are not easily deducible from other uses of their components. Thus, *blowing one's own trumpet*, meaning 'boasting', is an idiom in English.

The word *lexis* suggests such a series as *lexicon/lexical/lexicography/ lexicographer*, and these words suggest *dictionary/diction/word/vocabulary* and so on. In a dictionary the morphemes of a language are arranged in alphabetical order. It is possible, however, to think of words as arranged according to their meaning, in **sets**, whose members have semantic associations. Just as the systems of grammar impose limits of choice on the encoder of messages in the language, curb excessive originality and thus make what is said intelligible to decoders, so sets of words relating to areas of human experience impose limits on choice of vocabulary, for sets are words arranged round a central nucleus which has a core of meaning related to them all. Thus words like *family*, *father*, *mother*, *son*, *daughter*, *uncle*, *aunt*, *sister*, *brother*, *grandmother*, *cousin*, etc., all have something to do with *kinship*. When a word is taken out of its set and used in a new way it becomes metaphorical, and ideas associated with it become transferred to another context. The word *choir* could belong to some such set as *nave*, *apse*, *transept*, *aisle* and other words connected with church architecture, but when Shakespeare refers to boughs of trees in autumn as 'Bare ruin'd choirs where late the sweet birds sang', he gives it a new meaning in a new context.

# Exercises 23

**1** Consider these sentences:

'This year's snazel harvest is the lowest on record.' 'She was wearing a new snazel-green summer dress.' 'The snazel of Laos is said to be the finest of all that is grown in South East Asia.' 'These vegetable oils, widely used in cooking and as an ingredient in some cattle foods, are made from crushed snazel seeds.' 'Pushing aside the heavy fronds of snazel, the petals of whose yellowish-green flowers fell about him, he came at last to a clearing in the jungle.'

Using only the information given above, write a dictionary article, as full as possible, on the word *snazel*. Compare your dictionary article with the *Oxford English Dictionary*'s articles on *hemp*, *jute* and *sisal*, and say in what respects your article is lacking and why.

Consider and report on the ways in which we normally become acquainted with the meanings of words. Do you learn to know the meaning of, say, *adiabatic* in the same way as you learn the meanings of such words as *chair, table, window, apple*? What kinds of words have you learnt the meanings of from dictionaries, from definitions given by teachers of some special subject; what kinds of words do you normally never look up in dictionaries? Consider your own experiences and compare them with those of your colleagues.

**2** Consider the following compounds. Find or invent intelligible sentences containing the compounds and also the morphemes out of which they are composed: e.g., 'They lived in a flat on the ground-floor'/ 'The first floor is twenty-five feet above the ground.' Discuss the relationships of pronunciation and accent in spoken form (phonic substance) and hyphenation or absence of it in written form (graphic substance).

landlady, whitewash, chairman, boiling-point, bridesmaid, turbo-jet, crossword, centre-forward, horse-chestnut, paperback, tongue-tied, bed-sitter, countryside, birthplace, power-station, oversimplify, first class, second-hand, broken-hearted, coal-mine, one-sided, tooth-brush, sunset, off-shore, sandstone, city-dweller, broadcast.

How can you deduce the meaning from the order in which the morphemes are combined? What is the difference between *boat-house* and *house-boat*? Why do we speak of 'freedom-loving nations' and not '*loving-freedom nations'?

**3** Consider these sentences and the questions which follow them:

'Cleopatra was queen of Egypt, and the use of cosmetics reached a zenith in her reign.' *Zenith* is a scientific technical term whose meaning has been extended. How many meanings has it now? Can you find other examples of technical terms which have become 'popularized'?

'Of recent years British artists seemed to commit themselves too complacently to the romantic vision.' What do you understand by *romantic vision*? Consider the paradigmatic relations of each of these words.

'The problem of Japan loomed high on the horizon of those empowered to make decisions.' What exactly, do you think, is the 'horizon of those empowered to make decisions'? What does *high* mean? What does *loomed* mean, with its associated idiom *loomed large*?

'Food for the internationally-orientated palate comes too in the first précis-length recording of Wagner's *Flying Dutchman* to be made from the vast banquet that is Beyreuth.' Discuss the metaphors in this sentence.

'Thus the total vorticity, and hence the circulation, will have a steady value if the amount of vorticity shed is zero.' (From an article on aerodynamics) *Vorticity* is not to be found in any easily available dictionary, so how would you set about learning its meaning, if it has one?

'Four hundred years have not lessened the sense of ingenuity with which, like all great artists, Dowland surmounted the limitations of his medium and, indeed, turned them to account.'

Explain how 'four hundred years' can lessen a 'sense of ingenuity', if they can. Is *artists* used in the same sense as in the sentence above, and if it is, or is not, how do you know? Is *turn to account* a cliché?

# Chapter 24

# Idiolect, Dialect, Register

Language is used only by human beings. It can be considered from the point of view of the human beings who use it or from the point of view of the uses to which they put it. The first way of considering language is interesting, but the second is probably more useful and fruitful for linguistic science.

An **idiolect** is his way of using language by an individual speaker, and since everyone of us is different from everybody else there are as many idiolects as there are speakers. Every idiolect exists in the environment of a **dialect,** which is a way of using language determined by the geographical region of upbringing of the user or the social status of a special class of people.

**Register** is language considered from the point of view of the uses to which its uses put it, and is a complex but important matter. As we have seen, every use of language exists in a **situational context,** or set of circumstances which calls it forth. This context will determine what the particular use of language is about, or the subject-matter of the utterance or utterances that make up the discourse, and this will dictate the kind of vocabulary used (the sets of words from which selections are made) and very often the kinds of sentences used. But human beings will be involved in this language activity—there will be speaker and listener or writer and reader. This fact will produce both medium and mode. The **medium** is the kind of language used, whether spoken or written, informal or formal, popular or learned, technical or non-technical, prose or verse, etc. **Tenor** is the manner of utterance dictated by the relationship between speaker and listener, writer or reader: adults speaking to children use language differently from when they are speaking to other adults; experts use language differently when speaking to laymen from the way they use it when speaking among themselves on the same topic; books on nuclear physics are not written in the same way as cookery recipes; Acts of Parliament do not use the same sort of language as advertisements for soap; and so on. The combination of these features, context, medium and tenor, will produce the **style** of the use of language in any particular register.

# Exercises 24

**1** A useful concept in dealing with the various kinds of uses of language is that of **redundancy**, which may be technically defined as the difference (in the arithmetical sense) between the theoretical total capacity of a code and the average of the amount of information conveyed by it. This can best be understood by thinking of the idea that no matter what is said about anything something more could be said. If some one asks me the way to a post office in a certain town and I say, 'Turn left by the traffic lights and it's on your right opposite the George Hotel', I have probably said enough. But I could have said a lot more—I could have used more of the resources of language. I could have given an exact map reference on several kinds of Ordnance Survey maps of Great Britain; I could have specified its exact distance in both miles and kilometres from some object in Amsterdam; or given its position relative to the Statue of Liberty in New York harbour and the main entrance to the Kremlin. And what is more I could have chosen various kinds of media in which to say all that—words of one syllable, very elaborate prose using the technical terms of surveying, alliterative verse in the manner of Swinburne, or in heroic couplets with a pun on the name of a British Prime Minister in every sixth line.

Efficient use of language is that which conveys the maximum of information with the minimum of resources, but in its normal uses language is rarely efficient, because of built-in redundancy and because the use of redundancy can make language so much more pleasant in use. An example of built-in redundancy is 'he says', where the morpheme -*s* colligating with *he* is not really necessary—'*\*he say*' would do just as well. And if a boy says to his girl-friend 'I love you' he has probably made efficient use of language, giving the maximum of information with the minimum of resources, but if he says 'I love you, darling' he has brought in redundancy. Nevertheless, the redundancy is something that the decoder of the message was delighted, we hope, to hear.

Literary uses of language are full of redundancy. Poetry, for instance, uses the sound of language—rhythm, rhyme, alliteration, assonance, onomatopoeia—as well as imagery, extension of the meanings of words, and intricacies of 'decoration' employed to embellish imaginatively the otherwise plain, factual, 'efficient' statement of the norm of prose. The constant bringing in of the redundancy of the language code into poetry, the booty of 'raids on the inarticulate', provides the source of perpetual originality and freshness.

There can, of course, be misuses of redundancy, when the communication channel becomes noisy, and an unfortunate, careless, inconsiderate use of language baffles the decoder. The author of 'Motorways involve a varied number of structures over their length, ranging in magnitude from major bridge structures to minor culverts', for instance, was so careless of what he was saying that he hardly said anything at all, and the confusions of thought apparent in the utterance show that the process of encoding was so inconsiderately undertaken that the resulting signal does not enlighten the decoder but merely irritates him.

Discuss this notion of redundancy.

# Chapter 25

# Stylistics

**Stylistics** is that part of linguistic science which studies and tries to account for the styles of various uses of language. Every use of language has some sort of style which is derived from its register. The ideas of context, medium and tenor, which are aspects of register, can lead us to the notion that behind every use of language there is a process of selection, from a wide or narrow range, going on when messages are encoded. This process can be called **screening**, a process which, when a message is encoded allows some linguistic elements to pass into the signal and debars others. The student of stylistics has to answer the question why only those particular elements in a discourse have been allowed. Having found the date or period of the discourse and its provenance, he can proceed to examine its screening to discover what items of the resources of the language have been allowed into the signals and why. To do this in a systematic way a fourfold arrangement of screens can be established.

The first is a **phonological screen**. If the discourse is spoken it can be examined in the light of dialect and idiolectal peculiarity. If the discourse is written, deviations from Standard English can be looked at and accounted for, and such matters as punctuation, typographical support, spelling, rhythm sound of words when read aloud, and so on, will have to be examined too. The problem here is to discover how the written form realizes the basic elements of speech, whether the written form exists as communication in its own right, and if so how the graphic substance expresses, or helps to express, the content. The second is a **grammatical screen**, where the methods of modification of nouns and verbs, the interrelatedness of sentences, and general matters of syntax and morphology, will have to be examined to see how they contribute, and why, to the meaning of the whole. The third is a **lexical screen**. Here the kinds of words used, the ways in which collocations, idioms and clichés relate to the register of the discourse, and the choice of words from appropriate sets, will all have to be examined and accounted for. The fourth is a **redundancy screen**. Considerations of register will affect the phonology, grammar and lexis of a discourse, but it is possible to conceive of a 'norm of utterance' against which, given the register, the redundancy of a discourse can be compared. Any sentence can be expressed in minimal morphemic form, according to one or another of the five basic types or transforms of three of them. This minimal morphemic form can then be compared with the original and the expanded form of the sentence can then have its elements accounted for and explained in this relationship.

In every discourse there will be a feature that arises from its register and which is called **cohesion**, which is a property of discourse by which phonological, grammatical and lexical items show interconnected reference. Phonological cohesion is shown in, among other things, dialect and in a consistency in graphic substance of relationships of punctuation and typographical support. Grammatical cohesion is shown by reference back (anaphora) of determiners and pronouns, inside individual sentences or in chains of sentences, and in the consistency of sentence structure itself. Lexical cohesion is seen in lexemes which refer back, and in the selection of words from sets appropriate to the subject-matter of the discourse.

# Exercises 25

1 Consider the stylistic features of the following sentences:

(a) The grey spectres of the second movement he moves fleetingly, pointedly past the ears and, from the last movement, he draws every emotional significance from the dark stumbling of the opening funeral march to the febrile lines of the allegro.

(b) The three bunnies sat up, quite still, for they wondered what the strange thing was.

(c) In restricted parts of streets, where the waiting of vehicles is limited to short periods, the Minister agrees that street trading is better avoided, though he sees no reason to exclude the possibility that a few traders might be found accommodation in suitable parts of such streets without undesirable consequences for traffic.

(d) Ricci leads the eye to the rise and fall of the hem-line with short-skirted suits jacketed by a man's shirt and over-coated with cold-excluding coats that reach a new low for hems—mid-calf—to meet up with coloured knee-socks.

(e) The result shown indicated that the wear on the slide valve was in excess of that of the packing rings for the piston valves, from which it was deduced that the frictional resistance offered by the valves was one sixth less in the case of the piston valves.

(f) In his tiny red-brick laboratory, set below the cliffs and looking out on to the bay where holiday-makers lounge all day in bikinis, the 39-year-old Dr Braurmann, one-time Austrian refugee from Nazi oppression, told me other facts in the curious life of the lobster.

(g) It was after Villa had taken an almighty hammering that Salt began the final work of destruction.

(h) If the bulk of the glass is assumed to contain a large number of trapping sites between quasi-conductors and valence bands, then it can be deduced that the most likely distribution of traps is of double expotential form, that is, many traps near the band edges and few in the middle of the band gap.

(u) She was no lady, but Charlie was her darling and she was Charlie's, and so she is graciously allowed to haunt Salisbury Hall, which is near St Albans.

(j) The sudden and temporary loss of confidence in sterling on two occasions during the first three months of the year was not due to any real deterioration in the United Kingdom's balance of payments; indeed, the underlying situation was probably improving all the time.

(k) To Clive Barrow it was just an ordinary day nothing unusual or strange about it, everything quite navel, nothing outstanly just another day but to Roger it was something special, a day amongst days . . . a red lettuce day . . . because Roger was getting married and as he dressed that morning he thought about the gay batchelor soups he's had with all his pals.

(l) As there is no adequate consumption survey for the whole of Thailand, food consumption in the recomputed account is based on an anthropological survey of consumption over a full year for one village only, the implicit assumption being that consumption patterns in this village are more or less representative of the country as a whole.

(m) The technique, briefly, involves the manufacture of sodium alginate, dissolving it in caustic soda and subsequent extrusion through a spinnerette into a bath of calcium chloride solution.

(n) It argues that the imagination of Christendom grasps reality only under Catholic forms; that Protestantism is the enemy not only of religion but of art; and that the mess we so often say we are in was caused by an attempt to replace what God and time have made irreplaceable for us, the faith by which we are alone able to understand human experience.

(o) On the island of Djerba a good lotus may now be hard to find, but it boasts one of the oldest synagogues in the world.

---

The following sentences are taken from newspapers and periodicals printed in Britain since 1960.

(a) Pompeii and its wall pictures disappeared under a hail of volcanic ash in A.D. 79.

(b) At Melton Mowbray, in some 350 acres of War Department meadow land, the RAVC nurses sick horses and has a splendidly up-to-date veterinary operating theatre and X-ray unit.

(c) The public debt shrunk from 1,300m. francs last month, but over the first eight months it increased by over 5,900m. francs, while the short-term foreign currency debt increased by 4,800m. francs to 17,600m. francs.

(d) Hardly a house in the central part of the town can have seen a lick of paint in the last fifty years.

(e) On the second day, Dr H. M Glass, M.Sc., Ph.D., F.R.I.C., Technical Director of the British Standards Institution, presented a paper on the standardization of the standard of living.

(f) The trouble with *cinéma-vérité* is that it all depends on how interesting your *vérité* is.

(g) After 25 years of making a great deal of money out of building ships the Swedes can afford to live off their fat until the boom returns.

(h) A Paris expert calls the autumn make-up the 'diaphanous look!'

(i) Adams has discovered that Love in real life *may* have *acted for* a landlord of Joyce's at the very address at which his fictional counterpart is the distaining landlord of 'Father' Bob Cowley.

(j) The effect is claustrophobic; you might be bound in reeds, or mermaid's hair, and dragged down, down, down into some blue lagoon or cave beneath the sea, like *La Cathédrale Engloutie* by Debussy . . .

(k) Only two new 12-metre yachts have been built in Britain in the past five years.

(l) After winning the 250 and 350 cc races and consolidating his leadership in both championship classes, he crashed in the 125 cc race and broke a collar bone.

(m) However, the *trou*, unfortunately, has nothing to do with British meals, but the *sabat* has, because, somewhere along the line of courses, it has been preceded by hors-d'oeuvre.

(n) The literature in *Trends in physical education*, especially books on the 'system-apostles', is generally not of a high scientific standard (hypotheses without foundation, vague concepts, etc.) but there are some exceptions.

(o) Between 1950 and 1961 the annual turnover handled by the retailers of Britain leapt from £5,000 million to not far short of £9,000 million, while the number of retail firms shrank by nearly 3,000.

(p) The name 'earthenware' lacks glamour, say the potters, and so they have chosen new names to lift earthenware onto the bone china bandwagon.

(q) He sees the entire supernaturalist scheme of things in what was originally a three-decker universe (Up to heaven, Down to hell) as mythological in character.

(r) Thanks to the new figures from the Board of Trade we know that in the first quarter of 1963 the insurance companies, the biggest institutional investors, put £73m. new money into fixed-interest stocks as compared with only £20m. in equities.

(s) Russian reading habits are changing rapidly with more translations, not only into Russian, but also into languages like Georgian, of west European literature.

(t) Because of the overriding character of the conflict over the role of manned bombers, arguments concerning the technical feasibility or even the expense (within reason) of the *Skybolt* project were basically irrelevant.

1 Consider these sentences from the point of view of typographical support and the ways in which punctuation, capitalization, italics, parenthesis, inverted commas, etc., are used to express meaning.

2 Make tape-recordings of some of the sentences and discuss how the same meaning as is given in graphic substance is expressed in phonic substance.

3 If you were asked to advise a foreign learner of English on how to deal with numbers in written English, what advice would you give?

## II

Discuss the following sentences, which are all taken from periodicals printed in Britain since 1960. Many people would object to the 'English' of them. On what grounds? Do they conform in most respects to the conventional uses of English, or do they set up their own conventions? Why should they conform? If they set up their own conventions is there any justification for their doing so? Is it possible that any are written in a dialect?

(a) Motorways involve a varied number of structures over their length, ranging in magnitude from major bridge structures to minor culverts. (Context: civil engineering)

(b) Apart from housing estates in London, the LCC have also taken under their wing 20 country towns for the building of over 50,000 houses. (Context: town planning)

(c) Most currently produced high precision mouldings are produced by relatively small specialized moulders and, compared with the general moulding field, the quantities tend to be less. (Context: industrial chemistry)

(d) Assuming, therefore, that the Company in question is a land-owning Company, the value of its chargeable land being at least equal to one fifth of the net value of all its assets, the next matter to consider is the requisites of the Company whose shares are being disposed of, in order that Section 4 should apply. (Context: financial interpretation of company law)

(e) Domestic lighting falls into four rough categories: specific lighting for reading, sewing; direct lighting for dining; overall lighting for kitchens, hall, stairs; and background lighting for subtle effects and general but unobtrusive light. (Context: electricity in the home—advice to suppliers of domestic electrical installations and appliances)

(f) Valuable lessons in hospital function and design are readily available by studying the numerous experiments carried out in other countries, particularly in the United States of America and Canada, where, in an endeavour to cope with problems of rising costs, and staff shortages, accompanied by continual increase in public demand for hospital facilities, over 1,000 new hospitals have been constructed since the end of World War II. (Context: architectural problems in hospital design) (g) In the case of manufacturing industry, the effect of the abnormal climatic conditions experienced during the opening months of the year was not thought to be great, the Board states, as the main contribution to the fall between the fourth quarter of 1962 and the first quarter of 1963 was in expenditure on plant and machinery which was down 9 per cent at 1958 prices seasonally adjusted; the fall in expenditure on new building work was only about 4 per cent. (Context: review of British trade)

**1** Make a lexical study of these words, considering their paradigmatic relations and meanings: *involve, currently, domestic, facilities.*

**2** Examine the grammatical cohesion in the sentences.

**3** Examine lexically these pairs of words and the sets in which the words are likely to be found: *magnitude/size, requisites/needs, numerous/ many, accompanied by/with, continual/continuous, constructed/built, climatic conditions/weather.* What considerations of style would lead you to prefer the first of each pair to the second or the second to the first?

**4** Examine in their contexts above the following collocations and comment on their use: *a varied number; have also taken under their wing; currently produced; in question; in an endeavour to cope with; hospital facilities; in the case of; seasonally adjusted.*

**5** Can you explain the meanings of these expressions? If so, state how. *the general moulding field; rough categories; subtle effects; between the fourth quarter of 1962 and the first quarter of 1963.*

**6** Read the utterances aloud and make a tape-recording. Which is easier to understand, the written or the spoken form, and why?

## III

The following utterances are taken at random from scientific and technological journals published in Britain since 1960. Their subject-matter ranges through physics, chemistry, biology, zoology and medicine. What features, phonological, grammatical and lexical, do they have in common that could be described as belonging to a 'scientific style'?

(a) A slight variation of the mechanical arrangement described above is often made in order to ease the mechanical problem of mounting the reflector adjusting mechanism on the body of the discharge tube.

(b) The input interface may be defined as 'the plane of interconnection which exists between the plant measurement devices and transducers and the data logging equipment'.

(c) Each parameter was expressed as a percentage of the internodal mean and thereafter the pooled data for the proximal and distal bulbs were plotted separately.

(d) The chromatophores are supplied with very fine nerve endings from the sympathetic nervous system, which in all vertebrate animals controls the involuntary actions such as the heart-beat or movement of the intestine.

(e) A suspension of NO-dimethylaporotioraminol iodide (0.5g) in N-sodium hydroxide (50 ml) containing permanganate (1g) was shaken during 1 hr.

(f) Equation (7) shows that the bowing decreases as $f$, whereas from equation (5) $\triangle t_{min}$ is independent of $f$; therefore it is advantageous to use lower frequencies; at present 15kc/s is the lowest conveniently available.

(g) When disintegrated cell preparations were treated with an inducer, the enzyme was formed only if the system was provided with adenine, quanine, cytosine and uracil—presumably to permit the formation of new RNA.

(h) Such claims as have been made (Toumanoff, 1956; Le Corroller,

1958) are based on the repeated passage of B. *cereus* through insect larvae and it is clear that Lepidoptera often carry latent crystal-former infections so that it is extremely difficult to be sure that the bacterium isolated from a larva is the same as the one administered to it.

(i) If there is any change in the shape or surface charge of the red cells, then their permeation through the lymphatic filter becomes impeded and an obstructive vicious circle ensues, the cells being forced into the extra-sinusoidal splenic tissue.

(j) The sensitivity with which minute amounts of radioactive tracers can be detected makes them extremely valuable in the location and measurement of liquid and gaseous leaks.

**1** Rewrite two or three of the utterances in the passive in the active voice. What differences do you notice? What difficulties are there in expressing the results of scientific work or statements about what has been discovered scientifically in the active voice?

**2** Describe the typographical support used in (e), (f) and (h), and discuss its value.

**3** List all nominal segments in the sentences and give a grammatical description of their structures. What is the difference, linguistically, between *the data logging equipment* and *equipment for logging the data*? Are there any semantic dangers in the structure of some of the nominal segments found above?

**4** Examine the following collocations in their contexts above, find other ways of expressing their meanings, and state what, if anything, linguistically, each contributes to the utterance in which it occurs: *a slight variation*; *it is advantageous*; *such claims as have been made*; *are based on*; *it is clear that*; *vicious circle*; *extremely valuable*.

**5** Account, if you can, for the use of *is* and not *are* in the last grammatical sentence of (f).

**6** Make a lexical study of these words, considering some of their paradigmatic relations, their meanings and uses in other contexts and registers: *mechanical, mean, sympathetic, suspension, bowing, passage, administered, sensitivity, location, cell.*

(a) When the Department of Education and Science decided to experiment on a new type of building for Sixth Forms, it searched the Southern half of England for a suitable grammar school. Its choice fell on Roseberry, a country grammar school for girls at Epsom. In one way this was surprising, for one might have expected the department to have plumped for a boys' school. In another way it was not, for girls' schools, both State and independent, have been more imaginative than boys' schools in turning to good account the new trend to stay longer at school. (*Sunday Times*, August 16, 1964)

(b) Homes are now so much smaller than they used to be, and there seems to be so much more to put in them, that the question often comes up whether space should be found for books. Why own them? Cannot they be got from public libraries? If not, they are bound to appear as cheap paperbacks that can be read and discarded. It is no use being shocked by such an attitude. There are moments when one does wonder why some books have stayed on one's shelves for years. (*The Times*, February 4, 1965)

(c) America, with a population of 192 million living in 50 States, has to-day just under 400,000 full-time law enforcement officers. This clumsy term has to be used rather than the simple word 'police' because they come in many shapes and sizes.

Law enforcement men include dedicated and highly skilled professionals. But at the other end of the scale one finds semi-literate armed hooligans, often openly corrupt, among elected sheriffs and deputy sheriffs in the backward rural areas of the racist South and the Far West.

The American sheriff is nowadays a somewhat less romantic figure than his fabled counterpart in cowboy films. He is an elected official who functions at county level—States being subdivided into these—and is paid by the county. Naturally if he wants to keep his job he is inclined to bend the law in such a way as to conform to the prejudices of his community. (*Daily Telegraph*, March 18, 1965)

**1** Use these extracts as material for the basis of a discussion of the concept of cohesion.

**2** Discuss the typographical support in each extract.

**3** Consider these collocations and state with reason whether you think any of them are idioms or clichés: *its choice fell on*; *in one way*; *turning to good account*; *it is no use being*; *there are moments when*; *just under*; *they come in many shapes and sizes*; *at the other end of the scale*; *his fabled counterpart*; *is inclined to*.

**4** Express the sentences of (a) in minimal morphemic form, and do the same with three or four sentences from (b) and (c). Compare results with the expanded originals. Decide which modifications can be regarded as part of the redundancy of the language and which not. What can you deduce from this about the style of each extract?

**5** Make a lexical study of the following words, considering paradigmatic relations and ranges of use of some variants in other registers: *type, imaginative, public, dedicated, romantic, official, naturally*.

He is, as a jazzman, vintage Chicagoan. And for one who has been through forty years of that lung-hammering music, Wild Will Davison, now touring Britain, has worn well. In his sixtieth year—dapper, slick-haired, grey-suited—he suggests a spry Mid-Western business man up for a convention.

He plays trumpet that way too; with that egregious self-confidence which the practitioners of American business exude. 'The cockiest, sassiest, even blowsiest trumpet style in jazz,' said John S. Wilson of him. The description is as appropriate as his birthplace: Defiance, Ohio.

He is, in no pejorative sense, an old-fashioned gentleman. His style may have limitations, notably in its lack of surprise once his mannerisms have become familiar, but he does his stuff with flair, showmanship and practised polish. His playing in low register is beautifully controlled, his high runs golden-toned, flawlessly simple in structure. And he flecks his work with a knowing wit which laughs at the schmaltzy side of the Condon-type jazz he has been part of for so long.

He is accompanied by Freddy Randall's Band, not perhaps the ideal partners for him, but a crunchingly good group of mainstream tearaways in their own right. Bruce Turner is playing excellent alto and clarinet—and his reincarnation with Ronnie Gleeves of the Goodman Quartet days is uncanny. Gleeves, punishing the vibraphone like a blacksmith, is quite exciting enough to be known henceforth as Lionel Hampton's doppel-ganger. (*The Sunday Times*, January 31, 1965)

**1** Make a lexical study of these words, considering paradigmatic relations where necessary and ranges of use of some in other registers: *vintage, convention, egregious, business, mannerisms, polish, runs, knowing, flecks, schmaltzy, crunchingly.*

How many of these words are metaphors in this passage? Explain them, and say how many of them are original and how many well-used or else vogue-words.

**2** Distinguish between two kinds of compounds among the following: *jazzman, lung-hammering, slick-haired, grey-suited, Mid-Western, self-confidence, birthplace, old-fashioned, golden-toned, Condon-type, mainstream, tearaways.*

**3** Examine these collocations: *one who has been through; has worn well; he plays trumpet that way; in no pejorative sense; he does his stuff; beautifully controlled; been part of for so long; not perhaps the ideal partners; in their own right.*

Consider these along with other collocations suggested in these applications and decide how far many of them are clichés or idioms. How far do collocations help to preserve the conventional usages of the language and curb excessive originality on the part of encoders of messages, so that users of language can just get on with the job of communicating with one another in the necessary daily affairs of life? Is excessive originality on the part of encoders only desirable in wit, literature, and language used for its own sake?

**4** What interpretation do you put, if any, on the last sentence of the passage above?

**5** Is the passage above written in a dialect? Discuss its stylistic features from this point of view.

The year under review experienced a further decline in the demand for British motor cycles on the home market, a trend which persisted throughout the whole year. This disappointment, after the encouraging signs of some improvement in trade which seemed possible in the spring, has made the task of eliminating the company's trading losses that much more difficult.

The consolidated Profit and Loss account shows a Group loss of £990,606. Although this was caused substantially by trade declining at a faster rate than reorganization could be accomplished, it should be noted that approximately £400,000 relates to non-recurring expenses of reorganization, the residual losses of the Indian Company, and writing down of stocks following the physical amalgamation of various factories.

During the year Norton Motors Ltd. and R. T. Shelley Ltd. were successfully integrated into the Group's other factories. The vacated factories were satisfactorily disposed of, whilst other premises in Birmingham were sold and leased back to the company on commercial terms. (Company report, Associated Motor Cycles Limited—*The Financial Times*, April 6, 1964)

**1** Make a lexical study of these words: *experience, eliminate, consolidate, substantial, physical, commercial*. Comment on the use of these words or variants of them in the extract.

**2** Give a grammatical description of these expressions: *a trend which persisted throughout the whole year*; *that much more difficult*; *by trade declining*. Can you account for the colligation £400,000 *relates*? What grammatical differences do you notice in the use of these words, *encouraging, eliminating, non-recurring, following*?

**3** Consider the grammatical and lexical cohesion of the extract.

**4** Are the following expressions idioms? *on the home market*; *it should be noted*; *written down*

Employers' representatives told the Government yesterday what changes in the proposed 'statement of intent' on productivity, prices, and incomes would help to make it acceptable to the governing bodies of their organizations.

Mr. Brown, Minister for Economic Affairs, demurred at some of their suggestions, but agreed to consider most of them. He is to have further talks with the T.U.C. leaders and will then offer both sides a revised version of the statement in the hope that they will sign it before Christmas.

Although the employers are still sceptical about the possibility of regulating prices, they are not opposing a reference in the document to machinery for revising prices and wages. Their main positive request yesterday was that it should state clearly that the joint aim is to make prices competitive and industry dynamic and, above all, to clear away the obstacles to higher productivity.

They have been impressed by the recent declarations of Mr. Gunter, Minister of Labour, that the attack on such obstacles is primarily the responsibility of managements. The British Employers' Confederation have been expressing this view for some time. But they want to be sure that the T.U.C. commit themselves to recognizing publicly that the obstacles are there and must be removed, so that employers can adduce trade union support if they meet obstructive tactics on their part when they try to get rid of outdated or restrictive practices. (*The Times*, December 2, 1964)

1 Discuss the grammatical and lexical cohesion of this extract.

2 Express the first two paragraphs in minimal morphemic form, compare with the expanded originals, and discuss stylistic features. Compare the style of this extract with the styles of some others in this book.

3 Use the language of the passage to find out what can be deduced about the ways of expressing tense in English.

**4** Make a lexical study of these words, considering paradigmatic relations and possible uses in other registers: *representative, productivity, positive, organizations, machinery, dynamic, higher, attack, view, adduce.*

**5** Are these collocations in any way idiomatic or metaphoric? *governing body; both sides; in the hope that; for some time; to get rid of.*

## VIII

Of all the fields of interior decoration, the longest to take in new trends is the carpet industry. The enormous amount of fibres used to make a carpet, plus other high production costs, makes them much more expensive than other furnishing fabrics. The consumer too has a hand in making the carpet industry slow to change: the housewife expects the carpet to live through two or three changes in the rest of the décor. Because of these factors carpet manufacturers cannot afford to take chances on what may turn out to be a fad rather than a trend.

There are signs, however, that several fashions have had the approval of the manufacturers. First, seaweed green and orange in all their variations are to be seen in carpet showrooms now. William Morris designs are there, too, either in their original form or adapted to suit the more simple styles of the present day. From Scandinavia the rya rug of long shaggy wool has established its popularity and is being produced in a wide range of designs and colours. Discreet and regular geometric patterns are finding their way on to a multitude of carpets and these are an ideal way to introduce a patterned carpet into a small house.

As in fabrics, large designs in carpets tend to use tonal variations rather than a wide range of colours to create their pattern. These adapt themselves better to the average-sized living room and make an extremely attractive background for modern furnishings. (Supplement to *Homes and Gardens*, April 1964)

1 Examine nominal segments in this and other passages where an adjective precedes a noun—*interior decoration, enormous amount, their original form*. How many different kinds of such structures can you find? Is there any difference between such a structure as *the carpet industry* and such a one as *tonal variation*? How would you deal with *William Morris designs*? Consider the limitation of choice imposed on encoders by the conventional use of adjectives; e.g., we can speak of *an elderly man* but not of *★an elderly building*.

**2** Compare the differences in the groups *the consumer* and *the housewife* in the extract above with the groups *the employers* and *the obstacles* in the extract in 7. What are the semantic differences? How does one know that there are more than one consumer and more than one housewife? Or is this use idiomatic? How would you explain it to a foreigner learning English?

**3** Examine the grammaticality of the first two sentences of the extract. Is the question of whether or not the carpet industry can be considered one of the fields of interior decoration a grammatical one, a semantic one or a stylistic one? Can you account for *makes* in the second sentence?

**4** Make a lexical study of these words: *field, décor, factor, original, designs, popularity, average.* What do you understand by the use of the following words in the extract? *longest, plus, live, fad, now, multitude.*

**5** Make lists of homophones like *discreet* and *discrete.* Discuss their semantic relationship. How far can English orthography distinguish between the items of pairs?

## IX

Having roughly ascertained that the oscillator is working in the correct
frequency band—in the way previously mentioned—all that remains is
to effect a careful alignment using a meter. Either phones or a small
loudspeaker may be connected between C42 and B+, or an a.f.
amplifier may be attached.

A test oscillator or signal generator is required capable of giving a
modulated output (preferably f.m.) over the range of 85–100Mc/s.
This is set to 87·5Mc/s, and connected to the aerial socket of the receiver; moderate output will be required, say 10mV. The Volume
control should be adjusted so that the receiver does not emit too much
noise. Set the ganged capacitors to maximum (full interleaved) and
rotate the core of the oscillator indicator (L12) until a signal is heard.
If too loud reduce signal generator output. Tune the oscillator for peak
signal by means of the core. If the signal can be heard at two settings
of the core, select the position corresponding to the smaller value of
inductance.

Set the signal generator to 100Mc/s and the ganged capacitor to
minimum. Adjust the oscillator trimming capacitance until maximum
signal is heard. Next set the gang to the half-way position, and tune the
signal generator for maximum output in the receiver. Rotate the core
of the aerial coupling inductor and of the r.f. interstage transformer for
maximum volume. (*Practical Electronics*, December 1964)

**1** Without bothering about the technical terms in the passage, analyse
and discuss imperatives (commands, requests), as illustrated or exemplified above.

Explain the kind of difference in giving instructions as in the expression 'The volume control should be adjusted' and in 'Set the
ganged capacitor to maximum'.

**2** Examine the uses of the following words, both in the passage and in
their use in other registers, as in, say, 'a capable man', 'to the tune of

£500', ' a volume in the library', 'peak periods', 'apple-core', etc.:
*roughly, capable, tune, volume, peak, core, value, signal, gang, set.*

**3** Consider the grammaticality of the first sentence of the passage, and
discuss the immediate constituents of *having* and *using* and the segments
of which they are parts.

**4** Make a lexical study of the words of these pairs and consider words of
associated sets: *ascertain/find out, effect/bring about, select/choose, rotate/
turn.* Why should or should not the second of each pair be used instead
of the first? What would be the implications of a style which used the
second and not the first?

**5** Make lists of the technical terms used in various branches of science
and technology. Can you find any significant differences in those used
in biology and radio and electrical engineering, in chemistry and
physics, in civil engineering and the textile trade, and so on?

## X

73.—(1) A person who, by reason of the terms of an agreement or lease relating to any premises, is prevented from therein carrying out or doing any structural or other alterations or other thing whose carrying out or doing is requisite in order to secure compliance with a provision of this Act or of regulations thereunder which is, or will become, applicable to the premises, in order to comply with a requirement imposed by a notice served under section 30(4) or 35(2) of this Act or in order to enable effect to be given to proposals without contravention of a prohibition imposed by a notice served under the said section 30(4), may apply to the county court within whose jurisdiction the premises are situate, and the court may make such an order setting aside or modifying any terms of the agreement or lease as the court considers just and equitable in the circumstances of the case.

(2) Where the carrying out or doing in any premises of any structural or other alterations or other thing whose carrying out or doing is requisite as mentioned in the foregoing subsection involves a person having an interest in the premises in expense or increased expense, and he alleges that the whole or part of the expense or, as the case may be, the increase, ought to be borne by some other person having an interest in the premises, the first mentioned person may apply to the county court within whose jurisdiction the premises are situate, and the court, having regard to the terms of any agreement or lease relating to the premises, may by order give such directions with respect to the persons by whom the expense or increase is to be borne, and in what proportions it is to be borne by them and, if need be, for modifications of the terms of any such agreement or lease so far as concerns rent payable in respect of the premises as the court considers just and equitable in the circumstances of the case. (*Offices, Shops and Railway Premises Act*, 1963, H.M.S.O.)

1 Explain the reasons for the presence of all the clauses in the two sentences above.

2 Consider and comment on the grammatical function of the following and relate the function to the context above: *by reason of*; *in the circumstances of the case*; *as the case may be*; *therein*; *in order to*; *thereunder*; *situate*; *with respect to*; *if need be*.

3 Consider and comment on the use of the word *thing* in the two sentences above.

4 How would you describe the stylistic features of this extract?

5 Compare the style of this extract with that of other passages in books on science, logic, philosophy, etc., where precise definition and exact tools of analysis are needed. How far can such language exist in spoken form?

## XI

The Speaker took the Chair at 11 o'clock.

MR MAUDLING (Barnet, C.) said he had sought to put down a private notice question to the Prime Minister, which he believed was in order, about a matter of considerable urgency and importance, namely whether the Foreign Office adviser was being allowed to accompany . . .

The SPEAKER: It is not in order to repeat the terms of a private notice question which has not been allowed.

MR MAUDLING: Without attempting to repeat the terms, although the substance is well known, has the Prime Minister offered to make a statement on this? If not, what else can I do about it?

The SPEAKER: The Prime Minister has not to my knowledge offered to make a statement.

MR MACLEOD (Enfield West, C.): This question of position and status of this man reflects directly on the good faith of the Prime Minister in his statement yesterday.

If questions are to be disallowed, can we have an assurance that you do not regard it as part of the function of the Chair to protect the Government from proper questioning by the House? (Ministerial cries of "Oh").

The SPEAKER: The right hon. gentleman must make it quite plain that he is not seeking to cast any reflection upon the impartiality of the Chair—(Ministerial cries of "Withdraw")—because he will be perfectly entitled to do that, but not by way of question to the Chair. It would require a substantive motion. I should therefore ask him to make it clear that that was not his intention.

MR MACLEOD remained seated during repeated Ministerial cries of "Withdraw". (*The Times*, July 10, 1965)

1 This extract attempts to reproduce in writing a situation in which the language activity was largely spoken. Describe the function of

typographical support in the extract, giving an account of the functions of capital letters, parentheses, dashes, full stops, double inverted commas and any other features which seem of interest, showing how they contribute to the meaning of the whole.

2 The first and last sentences of the extract describe some extra-linguistic activity in the situation. What is the relationship between this extra-linguistic activity and the language activity itself, and what is the difference between the two kinds of extra-linguistic activity described?

3 What is your opinion of the writing *Oh* as a phonetic transcription of the Ministerial cries?

4 Mr Maudling's opening statement is given in reported (indirect) speech—a sentence of STO type with a nominal clause as object. Rewrite it as you think Mr Maudling actually spoke it, or better still make a tape-recording of it so that intonation can be heard. Discuss the question of the ambiguity of the clause *which he believed was in order* (Does it refer to the private notice question or Mr Maudling's having sought to put it down?), and try to decide whether the intonation of the spoken medium can resolve the ambiguity.

5 Make a lexical study of the words *considerable, substance, reflection,* and the form-class correspondences of their paradigmatic variants— *consider, consideration, substantial, substantive, reflect, reflector,* etc.—and examine the uses of some of these words in collocations, as in *a considerable amount, a substantial sum, on further reflection,* etc.

6 Examine the following collocations and among them distinguish idioms, clichés and what might be technical expressions peculiar to the register of the extract: *to put down; a private notice question; in order; not to my knowledge; the good faith, to cast a reflection upon; by way of question; make it clear that.*

7 Discuss the polysemy or multiple meaning of these words: *notice, order, prime, chair, house, plain, term.*

8 Make an IC analysis of the first sentence of Mr Maudling's second speech. What is your view of the grammatical cohesion of the phrase *without attempting to repeat the terms?*

9 What can this extract indicate of the differences between spoken and written English?

## XII

When designers incorporate rotating components in precision machines, accurate positioning and high performance can be obtained by the use of radial antifriction bearings incorporating balls, rollers, or combinations of both. In some instances, too, gases and magnetism are being used with radial bearings.

Antifriction linear systems have also been developed to provide equivalent effectiveness. The problems presented by friction in linear motion have become particularly severe with the increasing adoption of numerical control and machine automation. Although equipment is becoming heavier and more complex, it must comply with minimum friction, close-tolerance, and accurate positioning requirements at increasing speeds.

Until comparatively recently the solid metal bushing and shaft, the flat bed, and the V-way were the accepted guiding and supporting arrangements. Although many of these systems provided the best solution available at the time, and gave reasonably good performance initially, with continued use, friction, stick-slip movement, wear of mating parts, loss of accuracy, power requirements, and maintenance costs all increased.

Some 15 years ago, Thomson Industries, Inc., Manhasset, N.Y., U.S.A., developed linear antifriction ball bearings to help alleviate problems of linear motion friction. These bearings, known as ball bushings, have since been utilized in connection with round shafting to replace flat sliding components. Such precision antifriction linear systems have proved very effective where unlimited travel or repetitive reciprocation is required. They incorporate recirculating ball circuits which reduce friction in much the same manner as do balls in radial bearings. The current design, however, is only suitable for applications where individual bearing loading does not exceed 3,800 lb. weight.

In effect, the use of round shafting in combination with linear ball bearings for light- to medium-load precision machine application, established the principle of 'antifriction round ways'. (*Machinery*, January 20, 1965)

1 The register here is engineering technology. An engineer is writing about developments in the design of American machine tools, and he expects that his readers will be other engineers. How many of the technical terms used are self-explanatory to the layman, and how can the meanings of any other be deduced from the context?

2 What features of style, do you think, are influenced by, or are the result of, the exclusively written medium?

3 Consider the relationship of sentences which use parts of the verb *to be* in their verbal groups with those sentences which do not. Rewrite two or three of the passive sentences in the active voice, and compare the results with the original. Which are the more effective in the given register, and why?

4 Examine the polysemy or multiple meaning of these words and their particular meanings in the passage: *high, severe, solid, systems, travel, principle.*

5 Make a lexical study of these words, considering their paradigmatic relations and possible uses in other registers: *incorporate, performance, numerical, automation, complex, alleviate, current, established.*

6 Examine the cohesion of the passage. Is the first paragraph superfluous in this respect?

7 Consider these collocations and discuss their usefulness to the writer in the register in which he is writing: *high performance; until comparatively recently; at the time; reasonably good; in combination with; in effect.* Would you, or not, describe such collocations as *by the use of; the problems presented by; some x years ago; have proved very effective* as a kind of necessary 'shorthand' appropriate in the particular register?

8 Make an IC analysis of the last sentence of the third paragraph. Why is it that only lexical considerations can resolve the ambiguity in the sentence?

9 Consider the compounds and their use in the passage: *close-tolerance, V-way, stick-slip,* etc. Are there any instances where there might be compound words which the punctuation does not indicate?

10 Discuss the function and use of words in the passage which have the formal characteristics of present or past participles or gerunds.

## XIII

The first question to arise is whether any of the medieval narrative strength is absorbed into Wyatt's lyric. That is, did any literary osmosis take place in the mind of a Tudor courtly lover who admired Chaucer and himself wrote love poetry? For Wyatt, *The Knight's Tale* is an English classic which, in two poems, he echoes verbally. The borrowing of phrases, though an essential guide to the student, is, however, unimportant compared with the possible borrowing of attitudes and styles. Possibilities cannot be transformed into certainties, and, in my opinion, the relationship of Wyatt to Chaucer is best treated in terms of *affinity* and *guidance*. Their relationship may, indeed, fall outside the legitimate sphere of literary debts and influences. Wyatt's few biographical poems show that, at least sometimes, his chief source was life, not books, and this is likewise true of Chaucer, as it is of any great poet. I would suggest, nevertheless, that Wyatt was guided in his use of experience, not only by experience itself, but by the Chaucerian precedent. In particular, he is a Chaucerian student of the relation between experience and conventional behaviour or doctrine.

The biographical poem describing Wyatt's ill May days asks what *does* happen to one individual as distinct from what is supposed to happen or what happens to people in general. The sonnet is, in many ways, a synthesis characteristic of the best of Wyatt. For, while its mainspring is personal experience and its form Italian, its diction is Chaucerian; so too are the conventional terms that go with that diction. (Thomson, Patricia, *Sir Thomas Wyatt and his Background*, Routledge and Kegan Paul, 1964)

1 The register here is literary scholarship. Examine the following words and any modification of them, and use them as a basis for a description of the cohesion of the passage: *absorbed, osmosis, echoes, borrowing, relationship, sphere, source, nevertheless, particular, poem, sonnet, its.*

**2** Examine the following collocations and explain their necessity, even though some of them may be clichés, to the author's purpose, and therefore style, in this register: *That is*; *in my opinion*; *at least sometimes*; *in particular*; *in many ways*. In what ways do the following words assist this same purpose? *however, indeed, nevertheless*

**3** In what ways does typographical support assist in the cohesion of the passage?

**4** Give a grammatical description of the following items: *to arise*; *For Wyatt*; *compared*; *as distinct from*; *For*.

**5** Make a lexical study of the following words, examining paradigmatic relations and possible ranges of use in other registers: *narrative, absorbed, courtly, classic, essential, affinity, debts, precedent, doctrine, mainspring, diction*. Show how the meaning of some of these words is restricted by the author, so that possible ambiguity is avoided.

**6** What do you understand by the following? *narrative strength*; *literary osmosis*; *legitimate sphere*; *ill May days*

**7** Compare the verbal groups with the nominal groups or segments in this extract, and explain how and why the nominal groups or segments carry most of the total information conveyed. How are such verbal items as *take place, may, indeed, fall outside, would suggest* used, and how far can they be regarded as neutral signals of sentence form rather than lexemes with full referential meaning?

**8** Examine the possible polysemy or multiplicity of meaning of these words: *to arise, echoes, borrowing, attitudes, styles, terms, source, synthesis*.

**9** In scientific prose there is an absence of 'author-involvement'. Explain why the deliberate author-involvement of this passage—*in my opinion* and *I would suggest*—is not only unobtrusive but necessary.

**10** This extract uses the resources of language widely, but does not use any unnecessarily. Do you agree with this view?

## XIV

Mahler has for half a century been accused of orchestral bombast, or orchestral elephantiasis, of reckless piling of instrumental Pelian on Ossa. And circumstantial evidence admittedly can be got together making a plausible case for the prosecution, despite his quite aggressive insistence on counterpoint, his often angular line. A single glance at the scores of the Fifth, Sixth and Seventh Symphonies, or at the inner movements of the Ninth, shows the music as if under an X-ray, bones and criss-cross nerves, contrasting strongly with the well-fleshed harmonic coverings revealed by a Brahms score. But in the same symphonies, in the slow or slower movements, you will find strings yearning with nuance, the composer's expression marks almost hectically numerous. The violins stretch to the heights, the basses grope in the depths, while the woodwind play plaintively in between. Always the Mahler ambivalence as in the life of the man himself. Problem child and at the same time a musical thinker and an orchestral magician! He can be so restrained of tone that sometimes a vast Mahler canvas seems suddenly vacant, untenanted except for a few instruments seeking to find a tonal centre. Then pandemonium breaks out in brass and timpani; the entire tonal structure collapses, as at the end of the first movement of the Second Symphony. Yet Mahler's sonorities are seldom weighty or colossal because of thick blocks of harmony. The tumult is one of contending parts or of rhythms suddenly entangled.

When all is said and done, when all the Mahler storms have come and gone, we are compelled time after time to stress the fact that the main feature is the clearness and exposed identity of the scoring. Mahler was the first symphonic composer to make nearly every instrument a protagonist speaking in its own voice. Berlioz pointed the way to this kind of individualisation; Mahler coming later, and as a conductor in a position to learn every trick of the trade up to the latest moment, was able to enlarge his tonal encyclopedia and more and more give the significance he needed to his instrumental dramatis personae. (Cardus, Neville, *Gustav Mahler: his Mind and Music*, Gollancz, 1965)

**1** The register here is musical criticism. What do such expressions as *orchestral elephantiasis, well-fleshed harmonic coverings; thick blocks of harmony* tell you about the difficulties of writing about musical experiences? Are there any other features of the passage which also indicate these difficulties? Examine books, periodicals and any sources you can find for criticism of the arts other than literature, and discuss the problems of trying to express in language reactions to and experiences of what has been expressed in other media.

**2** Consider and discuss the cohesion of the passage. How far is it achieved by words in the set you would expect to find—*orchestral, instrumental, counterpoint, score*, etc.—and how far by other means?

**3** Examine and discuss the following collocations and the way in which the author makes use of them: *circumstantial evidence; case for the prosecution; the life of the man himself; problem child; when all is said and done; time after time; every trick of the trade.* How many of these are idioms and how many clichés?

**4** Discuss the use of metaphors in the passage, and the part played in their use by these words: *bombast, case, bones, nerves, stretch, grope, play, canvas, untenanted, protagonist, encyclopedia, dramatis personae.*

**5** Make a lexical study of these words: *instrumental, aggressive, scores, movements, nuance, expression, magician, restrained, weighty, colossal, individualisation, significance.*

**6** Consider and discuss the verbal groups in the order in which they occur in the passage. What kind of verbal groups could be put in the two utterances which have no verbal groups? What is the effect of the passage's not having verbal groups in those two utterances?

**7** Express the first three utterances of the passage in minimal morphemic form, and compare with the expanded originals. What is the effect of the modification?

**8** How far is much of this passage concerned with the use of language for its own sake rather than for telling the reader anything about Mahler?

**9** What meaning do you give to these expressions in their context above? *angular line; a single glance; you; yearning with nuance; almost hectically numerous; heights; depths, a musical thinker; we.*

**10** Compare and contrast this passage with another given in this book, and discuss the differences.

## XV

Consider and discuss the ideas presented in this passage:

The built-in redundancy of the use of language is a safeguard against the excessive originality of encoders; without the 'rules' of language, the pre-arrangement of the code, there would be little or no means of contact between man and man through language. At the same time, redundancy offers encouragement to those who wish to be original. What has not yet been said deserves as much consideration as what has been said already; the kinds of ways of using language that we don't habitually use in our ordinary everyday communicative acts are just as important as the routine utterances and usually far more exciting. The redundancy of a language, or that part of it which is of such improbable use that it never achieves average usage, is not for that reason of impossible use, and it is the source of literature. Poetry, drama and fiction rarely say anything that is new; they keep on repeating old ideas about man and his relations with his environment, and deal with perennial themes of his continually striving to assert himself, of his love and hate, folly, adventure, death, evil, disasters and triumphs, and all that makes him civilized and what he is; but all the time poetry, drama and fiction speak about these topics with ever-renewed originality of insight that is obtainable only through language. It is only by means of repeated exploitation of the language's redundancy—'raids on the inarticulate'—that literature is created. Poetry, drama and fiction combine into a whole three aspects of man's living; they are language used as a form of playing, of not working, of abandoning, for the moment, the responsibility of being alive; they are language used as exploration, of finding out everything about human life that there is to be found; and they are language used as a kind of revelation, a way of thinking and feeling, of sensuous apprehension of reality.

They do this chiefly by means of images, by bringing together two apprehensions of reality that are normally incompatible and using one of them to illuminate the other. All images, considered as uses of words that make comparisons, are metaphorical in character. It is simpler, however, to make a distinction between a syntagmatic structure that uses *as* or *like* and a special way of using what in most cases is a word, and to call the one a simile and the other a metaphor. Some writers on these matters would include them under the general head of 'polysemy' or 'multiplicity of meaning'. There is no objection to such a procedure, as there is none, if one wants a lot of names for minor distinctions, to the introduction of other names for what are supposed to be other figures of speech. For instance, metonomy (or using the name of an 'attribute' of a thing for the thing itself, as *the stage* for the profession of acting) or synecdoche (or using the name of a part for the whole, as *canvas* for a picture painted on canvas) are really only kinds of metaphors, in that, one supposes, the idea of the stage might be part of the connotation of the word *actor* and that of canvas part of the connotation of *the art of painting*. But these kinds of uses enter so deeply or widely into the language only in this way—through people having associated ideas of things, memories of them, feelings about them.

There are, of course, plenty of ways of playing with words which have been given the names of various figures of speech, and all of them are interesting. The question of imagery, however, is that of the integration of language with life. If some one says 'I saw a programme on television last night', he is, presumably, recounting no more than a fact of history; but if he says, 'I saw a lousy programme on television last night', he is recounting a fact of history and something else. His inelegant diction, the low modification injected into the plain statement of fact, is the vehicle of emotional attitudes and ways of responding to the world which make him interesting as a person. His disgust at the programme he saw, conveyed by the word that was used as a metaphor, even though a hackneyed one, is the kind of thing that continually enriches life and language with the splendours and degradations of our human condition. 'The business of art', said D. H. Lawrence, 'is to reveal the relation between man and his circumambient universe, at the living moment. As mankind is always struggling in the toils of old relationships, art is always ahead of the "times", which themselves are always far in the rear of the living moment.'

The greatest of the arts that use language is poetry. In prose the expression of the same notion or 'message' in two different ways is a matter of style, and the fact that the same message can be expressed in at least two different ways ('Dear Sir, I have the honour to inform you' or 'Jeeze, boss, get a load of this') shows that the form can be separated from the content. This is not so with poetry, where the needs of form have a great effect upon the content, and where the transmission of the message is not the prime consideration. Different kinds of metres have been traditionally assigned to different genres (heroic verse for epics, lighter kinds of verse forms for lyrics, and so on), or different existing forms have been used for different kinds of experiences (consider, say, sonnets and odes in English literature). The language of poetry differs from that of prose largely because poetry calls upon all the resources of language, phonological, grammatical and lexical, and does so primarily in the spoken medium as distinct from the written. (Orthographic experiments such as the 'eye-rhymes' of Edmund Spenser, the printed 'shapes' of George Herbert or Dylan Thomas, or various attempts at typographical artistry, can be regarded as 'sports' or 'deviations of the deviant'.) At the phonological level, poetry deviates from the 'norm' of prose in that it shows a 'principle of periodicity', a distinctive rhythm, not of course always the same, which is poetry's basic ingredient. This rhythm is essentially heard, and not, like the rhythm of painting or architecture, seen. It can be, and often is, embellished by various acoustical devices such as rhyme, assonance, alliteration, onomatopoeia, and the management of the length and pitch of syllabic elements. At the grammatical level, poetry can deviate from the norm of prose by not always being grammatical; but normally different styles of poetry will show different grammatical peculiarities—some styles will echo the rhythm by a relatively more frequent use of, say, nominal groups, than others, or in the complexities or lack of complexities in modification, inversion, and so on. At the lexical level poetry deviates from the norm of prose in its bolder use of polysemy and in its daring to 'disturb the universe' by not stating the obvious. Instead of talking about the 'faithful men who followed me' poetry says 'The hearts/That spaniel'd me at heels'. Poetry does not exist for the sake of the message; it exists for its own sake. It is language-music because it must be heard; and at the same time it is just language, not because of what it says (for it has all been said before), but because of the way it says it.

# Index

active voice, 30
adjectival behaviour, 53
— clause, 57
adjective, 64
adjunct, 28, 41
adverb, 67
adverbial behaviour, 53
— clause, 57
— sentence adverb, 29
allomorph, 67
allophone, 13
analysis, 34, 43, 47
apposition, 56

base, 67
behaviour, 53
bound morpheme, 42

case, 73
class, of forms, 60, 63, 70
clause, 52, 56, 57
cliché, 80
code, 1
cohesion, 88
colligation, 73
collocation, 80
communication, 1
commutation, 14
comparative, 71
comparison, 71, 74
complement, 23, 27
compound, 80
conjunction, 67
consonant, 14
constituent, immediate, 43
context, 47, 84
contoid, 10
contrast, 13, 37

decoder, 1

definition, 8
determiner, 64
diachronic study, 7

encoder, 1
expansion, 28

finite verb, 77
finitude, 67, 77
formal characteristics, 22
formal meaning, 19
form-class, 60, 63, 70
function, 8, 37
functor, 40, 41

gerund, 77
grammar, formal, 49
grammaticality, 47
graphic substance, 2
group, 23

head, 28, 41

IC Analysis, 43, 47
idiolect, 84
idiom, 80
immediate constituent, 43
— analysis, 43, 47
imperative, 76
indicative, 76
infinitive, 67
inflexion, 42, 71
informant, 19
information, 1
intensifier, 75
interrogative, 67
intransitive, 23, 27

language, 4
lexeme, 40, 41

lexicography 8
lexis, 8, 80
linguistics, 7
linkage, 67

meaning, 8, 19
medium, 84
message, 1
metalanguage, 9
minimal pairs, 14
modification, 41
mood, 76
morpheme, 7, 37
— bound morpheme, 4
morphology, 7, 73, 76

nominal behaviour, 53
— clause, 57
— segment, 55
noun, 63
number, 73

object, 23
operator, 67

paradigm, 27, 42
paradigmatic relations, 80
participle, 77
passive voice, 30
person, 76
phoneme, 7, 11, 13
phonetics, 7, 10
phonic substance, 2
phonology, 7, 11, 13
phrasal verb, 69
phrase, 52
position, 55
preposition, 64
pronoun, 64
pronunciation, 12
— Received (RP), 12

Received Pronunciation, 12
redundancy, 85

referent, 8
referential meaning, 19
reflexive, 75
register, 8, 84

screens, 87
segmentation, 18, 19, 51
semantics, 8, 19, 80
sentence, 18, 22, 23, 27
sentence adverb, 29
sets, 80
sign, 1
signal, 1
speech, 10
speech-community, 4
stability, 14
structure, 7, 18, 22, 26, 59
style, 8, 85, 87
subject, 23, 27
subordination, 67
surbordinator, 67
substance, 2
substitution, 18, 19, 51
syllable, 14
synchronic study, 7
syntagma, 27
syntagmatic relations, 80
syntax, 7, 18, 22, 26

tenor, 84
transforms, 30
Transformational Grammar, 31
transitive, 23, 27
typographical support, 45

verb, 23, 27, 53, 67, 69, 76, 77
verbal behaviour, 53
— segment, 67
vocal organs, 10
vocative, 55
vocoids, 10
voice, 30, 77
vowel, 14